EXPRESS YOURSELF!

EXPRESS YOURSELF!

INTERMEDIATE ENGLISH CONVERSATION

Trish Shannon
Los Angeles Community Adult School

McGraw-Hill, Inc.
New York St. Louis San Francisco Auckland Bogotá
Caracas Lisbon London Madrid Mexico City Milan
Montreal New Delhi San Juan Singapore
Sydney Tokyo Toronto

This is an EBI book

Express Yourself!
Intermediate English Conversation

6 7 8 9 0 MAL MAL 9 0 9 8 7 6

ISBN 0-07-556986-8

Library of Congress Cataloging-in-Publication Data
Shannon, Trish.
  Express yourself!: intermediate English conversation / Trish Shannon.
— 1st ed.
    p.   cm.
  ISBN 0-07-556986-8
  1. English language—Conversation and phrase books.   2. English
language—Textbooks for foreign speakers.   I. Title.
PE1131.S47   1989
428.3'4—dc19   88-35593
                                                               CIP

Manufactured in the United States of America

Production: Marian Hartsough Associates
Text and Cover Design: Juan Vargas, Vargas/Williams Design
Illustrations: Valerie Winemiller
Typesetting: Etcetera Graphics

▦▦▦▦ CONTENTS

⊞⊞⊞⊞⊞ PREFACE TO THE INSTRUCTOR

Most ESL and EFL conversation books are based on the competencies (life skills) and/or functions (situational usages of language) needed to prepare students for the realities of real-life language production. *Express Yourself!* is unique in that it utilizes competency-based, communicative exercises to focus on the language of common human reactions to situations that occur in daily life. For example, rather than learning how to use the bus system and speak to the bus driver, students learn to describe their feelings when they miss the bus. The "expressive" vocabulary in *Express Yourself!* is geared toward improving the communication skills of your students, enabling them to articulate the full range of their experiences.

ORGANIZATION

Express Yourself! is divided into ten chapters based on ways of feeling, thinking, or acting. Each chapter begins with a picture story that presents a dramatic situation. Using the vocabulary cues if needed, students can "warm up" by telling the story from the pictures, individually or in groups. Next, prepare students to talk about their own feelings by asking them to describe the emotions of the characters in the story. Typically, they will find it difficult to describe the characters' responses to the events, or they will do so ungrammatically, searching for appropriate vocabulary. These preliminary narratives may be used as an informal pretest of their ability to talk about events on a level beyond that of straight narrative.

In the "Words and Expressions" segment, students are presented with the target "expressive" vocabulary of the chapter, which they will use in the exercises that follow. Note that the words and expressions are grouped according to meaning rather than alphabetically. Slang expressions are indicated; since this is a conversation book, informal as well as formal expressions are listed. To familiarize students with the pronunciation of the new vocabulary, model the example sentences and discuss meanings and usages as a group. You may want to use the example sentences for dictation the following day.

After students are acquainted with the new vocabulary, have them ask and answer questions in "Telling the Story," an oral follow-up exercise that provides them with controlled vocabulary practice. You may wish to go over several questions as a group and then have students finish the exercise in pairs. Although this is primarily an oral exercise, students may also write their answers for reinforcement of learning. In the section that follows, "Finishing the Story," students express their personal reactions to the story that opened the chapter.

The communicative exercises that follow, "How Do You Feel?," "What Do You Do?," and so forth, provide students with more practice in using the new vocabulary. These exercises can be completed in small groups or pairs. "Body Language" is a visual exercise that depicts physical reactions to situations in the stories. Students learn to describe these gestures and motions. In the exercise that follows, students discuss the cultural differences in body language in small groups. Keeping corrections to a minimum during these sessions encourages lively, spontaneous conversation among students.

The next segment, "Expressions and Conversations," contains three dialogues that present functions in context. Students should first repeat the dialogues after you and then practice them in pairs. You may wish to check for correct pronunciation, stress, and intonation. Following each dialogue one or more variations of the original expressions are presented, which are to be substituted when the exercises are repeated. After practicing intonation and pronunciation, you may wish to have students memorize and then act out these dialogues.

After gaining a degree of confidence in the use of the functions just presented, students improvise conversations in the advanced "Role Play" exercise that follows. For this exercise, you may wish to divide the class into groups of three, with one student in each group acting as director. Since the goal here is spontaneous language production, encourage quick, extemporaneous sketches. If you prefer more polished performances, it may be necessary to allocate an entire class period to creating the conversations, which students should write down and you may quickly correct before they are presented. Pairing reticent students with more vocal ones, whenever possible, can be an effective device for getting students to talk.

"One Step Beyond" presents a variety of game activities to round out the language-learning experience. The "Interview" challenges students to use the new vocabulary and information they have learned in order to answer a series of questions. In the thought-provoking "Problem Solving" segment that follows, students decide how they would respond to various situations related to the chapter topics.

Finally, the supplemental "Wordplay" section offers three written exercises — "Prepositions," "Sentence Completion," and "Parts of Speech" — designed to reinforce and expand various aspects of the material presented in the previous sections. These exercises focus on specific points of grammar and usage and may be assigned as homework.

ACKNOWLEDGMENTS

The author would like to acknowledge the following reviewers, whose comments — both favorable and critical — were of great value in the development of the project:

Susan Ansara, State University of New York at Stony Brook; Tibe Appelstein, Newbury Junior College, Massachusetts; Van Caliandro,

Bronx Community College; Martin J. Conroy, Los Angeles Community Adult School; Ann Creighton, Southgate Community Adult School; Deborah Deane, University of Akron; Lorelei A. DePauw, North Hollywood Community Adult School; Frank Diffley, American Language Institute, University of California at Riverside; Gloria Directo, Refugee Assistance Center of Kansas City, Kansas; Fraida Dubin, University of Southern California, Los Angeles; Joy Durighello, San Francisco Community College; Frances Finch, Evans Community Adult School, Los Angeles; Randy Fischer, Los Angeles Community Adult School; Suzanne Flynn, Massachusetts Institute of Technology; Ellen Garshick, American Language Institute, Georgetown University; Kim Gerould, Community Learning Center of Cambridge, Massachusetts; Anne Lindell Hagiwara, Eastern Michigan University; Nancy Herzfeld-Pipkin, American Language Institute, San Diego State University; Mary D. Hill, El Paso Community College; Glenn Hopkins, University C.A.S.; Mary Hurst, Belmont Adult School, Los Angeles; Patricia Johnson, University of Wisconsin, Green Bay; Gail Kellersberger, Intensive English Institute, University of Houston; Mark Landa, University of Minnesota; Nancy Lay, City College of New York; Elizabeth Merceron, Los Angeles Unified School District; Bet Messmer, Santa Clara Adult Education Center, California; Martha Pennington, University of Hawaii; Helen Polensek, Oregon State University; Kara Rosenberg, Palo Alto Adult Education, California; Stanley S. Sacks, LaGuardia Community College, New York; Kent Sutherland, Canada College, California; Mary Thurber, City College of San Francisco, and Stephanie Vandrick, University of San Francisco.

The work of the copyeditor, Pat Campbell; the artist, Valerie Winemiller, and the production coordinator, Marian Hartsough is also much appreciated, as are the comments and input of Elaine Kirn of West Los Angeles College on the initial material and the editing of Mary McVey Gill.

T.S.

CHAPTER 1

HAPPINESS

▨▨▨▨ JUNE'S GOOD LUCK

Look at the pictures and vocabulary words. Talk about what is happening in each picture.

1.

lottery

2.

audience / sign

3.

spin / wheel

4.

5.

6.

7.

▦▦▦ WORDS AND EXPRESSIONS

expression	example
be {**happy** / **glad** / **pleased**} **about** {+ VERB*ing* / something} (= have good feelings)	He's happy about {finding his wallet. / the trip.}
be happy for someone **be pleased with** someone or something	I'm happy for you! She's pleased with her new apartment.
feel {**great** / **fantastic** / **terrific** / **wonderful**} **about** {+ VERB*ing* / something} (= have very good feelings)	I feel great about {finding my new job. / the decision.}
feel on top of the world (= feel great)	I feel on top of the world because I passed the test.
be excited about {+ VERB*ing* / something} (= be full of positive energy)	I'm excited about {learning to drive a car. / the party.}
be enthusiastic about {+ VERB*ing* / something} (= be full of interest and desire)	I'm enthusiastic about {starting my new job. / my new apartment.}
be {**thrilled** / **overjoyed**} **about** something (= be extremely happy)	She's {thrilled / overjoyed} about the new baby.
enjoy {oneself / + VERB*ing* / something} (= get happiness from things or experiences; always: (a) reflexive or (b) used with an object)	(a) I always enjoy myself at parties. (b) I enjoy {eating good food. / funny movies.}
have {**fun** / **a good time**} {**with** someone / **at** an event} (= enjoy an experience)	I always have fun with my best friends. We really have a good time at weddings.
get a kick out of {+ VERB*ing* / something} (= really enjoy something)	I got a kick out of {seeing the photos. / his letters.}
be / **feel** {**lucky** / **fortunate**} **to** + VERB something (= have something good happen by chance)	I'm lucky to get this job. I feel fortunate to be healthy.

expression	example
surprise someone	*You surprised me. You're usually late, but today you're early.*
be surprised { **at** someone or something / **about** something / **to** + VERB something } (= do something unexpected)	*I am surprised* { *at you!* / *about his decision.* / *to hear that.* }
accomplish something (= do or complete something)	*We accomplished a lot in only two hours of work.*
reach } { **a goal** / **achieve** } { **something** (= accomplish something difficult)	*He's working hard to* { *reach his goal.* / *achieve success.* }
be proud of { someone or something / + VERB*ing* } (= feel good about someone or something for a special reason)	*I'm proud of* { *my team.* / *winning the game.* }
congratulate someone **on** something (= tell someone you are happy about his or her achievement or good luck)	*She congratulated me on my new job!*
celebrate { someone's birthday/anniversary / **with** someone / + VERB*ing* } (= have a good time for a special reason)	*He's celebrating* { *his birthday with his family and friends.* / *her winning the contest.* }

▓▓▓▓ TELLING THE STORY

Look at the picture story to answer these questions. Pay special attention to the words **in dark type**.

1. Why does June look very **happy**?
2. Are her family and friends **proud of** her? What are they doing?
3. Why is everybody very **excited**?
4. Does June look very **surprised** when she wins?
5. How do June's family and friends **congratulate** her when she wins?
6. Where do they go to **celebrate**? Do they **have a good time**?

▓▓▓▓ FINISHING THE STORY

1. How do you think June will spend the money?
2. Will her life be easier after she wins?
3. What will you do if you win the lottery?

▨▨▨▨ BODY LANGUAGE

A. Match each picture with a description of the action. Write the correct letter on the line.

1. _____ smile (at)

2. _____ shake hands (with)

3. _____ put one's arm around someone

4. _____ clap/applaud (for)

5. _____ make a toast (to)

6. _____ jump up and down and cheer
   (= shout words of encouragement)

B. Work in pairs. Cover the words. Look only at the pictures. Describe what each person is doing and why. (Make up your explanations.)

_____

EXAMPLE: Picture B
1. What's she doing?   She's smiling.
2. Why?   ...because she's happy.
          ...because it's her birthday, etc.

_____

C. In groups, talk about cultural differences. Answer these questions:

1. Do people in your culture show their feelings of happiness in the same way as in the pictures?

2. Do men in your culture show happiness in the same way as women?

3. In what other ways do you express happiness?

Summarize your discussion for the class.

▓▓▓▓ EXPRESSIONS AND CONVERSATIONS

A. Practice the following conversation with your partner. Use the appropriate body language to act out (dramatize) the situation.

MUSICIAN 1:   Jeff, <u>I'd like to introduce you to</u> our new singer, Laurie.

MUSICIAN 2:   <u>Pleased to meet you</u>, Laurie. I've heard a lot about you.

SINGER: <u>Nice to meet you</u>, too. Gee, <u>I can't wait to</u> start practicing with you.

MUSICIAN 2:   Same here. I think we're going to <u>enjoy</u> playing <u>together</u>.

B. Now practice the conversation again. Use different expressions for the underlined words. Have several different conversations.

EXAMPLE: [instead of] Pleased to meet you.
           [say] **Glad to meet you.**

▓ **Making Introductions**   (= telling two people each other's names for the first time)

I'd like to introduce you to _____.
I'd like you to meet _____.

▓ **Meeting for the First Time**   (= being introduced for the first time)

Pleased
Glad
Nice   } to meet you!
Delighted *(formal)*

▓ **Expressing Enthusiasm**   (= showing someone you are happy and excited about doing something)

I can't wait to
                        } meet them.
I'm { **eager to**   start playing.
        { **anxious to**

I think we're going to { **enjoy** playing (working) **together.**
                           { **get along well together.**

C. Practice the following conversation with your partner.

FAN 1: <u>Come on</u>, team! <u>You can do it</u>! Beat the Tigers!

FAN 2: Hey, Tigers! <u>Don't give up</u>! Fight back!

FAN 1: Yea, Lions! Play a little harder! Score again!
The Lions score again. Yea, we scored! <u>Nice going</u>, team!

Practice the conversation again. Use expressions from the following list instead of the underlined words.

▣ Cheering (= saying words of encouragement)

Come on!	**Hurray!**	**Nice going!** *(slang)*
Go!	**Yea!**	**Way to go!** *(slang)*
		Right on! *(slang)*

▣ Encouraging Someone (= giving support)

Don't give up!
Keep trying!

$$\text{You can} \begin{cases} \text{do it!} \\ \text{win!} \\ \text{score!} \\ \text{beat them (him, her)!} \end{cases}$$

D. Practice the following conversation with your partner.

TEACHER: And now <u>I'd like to propose a toast to</u> Young Soo. <u>Congratulations</u> on your scholarship*.

YOUNG SOO: Gee, thank you very much. <u>I can't tell you</u> how happy I feel today!

STUDENT: Nice going, Young! Good luck with your studies next year! We'll miss you!

YOUNG SOO: I don't know what to say. This is great! <u>I really appreciate</u> all your help and enthusiasm.

Practice the conversation again. Use expressions from the following list instead of the underlined words.

▣ Congratulating Someone

Congratulations
Nice going! *(informal)*
Good work!

▣ Making a Toast (= drinking to someone's health and happiness)

I'd like to propose a toast to _____.
Here's to _____. *(informal)*

---

*scholarship (n.) = a gift of money to pay for education

🞔 **Accepting Congratulations**

I really appreciate { your help.
                         your helping me.
I'm very grateful to you **for** your help.

I can't tell you
You have no idea } how happy I am!

E. Now role play the situations in this section. Use your own words and the appropriate body language. How do you feel in each situation?

🞖🞖🞖🞖 EXPRESSING YOURSELF

A. **How Do They Feel?** Find a partner. Ask and answer questions about the story at the beginning of the chapter. Use *feel*, *look*, or *act*.

EXAMPLE: **Picture 1**
   1. **How does June feel?**   **She feels excited.**
   2. **Why?** ...**because she may win the lottery.**

B. **How Would You Feel?** Work with your partner. Take turns asking and answering the following questions. Use the correct preposition: *about*, *with*, *on*, or *of*.

SITUATION: You have just gotten a promotion.

EXAMPLE: What are you happy _____? *(getting a promotion)*
   What are you happy about?   **I'm happy about getting a**
   promotion.

---

1. What are you surprised _____? *(getting a promotion)*

2. What are you glad _____? *(my new schedule)*

3. What are you excited _____? *(making more money)*

4. Who congratulated you _____ your promotion?
   (my friends)

5. Why are you enthusiastic _____ you new position?*
   (the money and the hours)

6. Who are you proud _____? *(myself)*

7. Who are you celebrating your promotion _____?
   (my friends)

---

*Remember: Use *because (of)* to answer questions with *why*.

C. **What Do You Say?** Use these expressions in your answers to the questions that follow.

We're very proud of you!

I'm delighted to meet you!

Boy, are you lucky!

I feel great!

Are you having a good time?

Did you enjoy your trip?

Congratulations! Let's go celebrate.

What an accomplishment!

I'm thrilled!

EXAMPLE: What do you say when you see someone you know at a party?
[say] **Are you having a good time?**

WHAT DO YOU SAY?

1. ...when you run into your friend after his or her vacation?

2. ...when your friend gets a better job with better pay?

3. ...when someone returns a lost wallet to your friend?

4. ...when your child gets an A on his or her report card?

5. ...when a friend introduces you to someone you always wanted to meet?

6. ...when you win a prize in a contest?

7. ...after you get a good night's sleep?

8. ...when a friend finally finishes a difficult job?

▨▨▨▨ ROLE PLAY

Work with a partner.
Choose one of the following situations.
Each student plays one role.
Read and think only about your role.
How do you feel?
Act out the situations. Use expressions from this chapter.
(Your teacher may ask another student to direct and give suggestions.)

Role A	Role B
1. You are watching a race. You are encouraging your friend Sam to win.	1. You are also watching the race. You are cheering for your friend Pat. You want her to beat Sam.
2. You have just passed a hard examination. Your friend is congratulating you.	2. Your friend has passed a difficult exam. You are congratulating him or her on his or her hard work.
3. You the proud parent of a new baby. Your friend is congratulating you.	3. You are congratulating your friend on the birth of his or her new baby.
4. (your own situation) ?	4. (your own situation) ?
5. You are a member of a school acting club. You are meeting a new actor joining the club for the first time.	5. You are introducing the new actor to one of the other members.

Role C = You are a new actor. You are excited about joining the acting
club.

6. You are at a party. Your friend is introducing her or his new boyfriend or girlfriend to you.	6. Your boyfriend or girlfriend is introducing you to his or her best friend for the first time.

Role C = You are introducing your new boyfriend or girlfriend to your
best friend.

INTERVIEW

Ask your partner the following questions. Take notes on the answers. (Your teacher may ask you to do this exercise in groups of three or four.)

1. Sometimes very small things can make people happy. Name four "little things" that make you happy.

EXAMPLE: [say] **A phone call from my friend makes me happy.**

---

2. In your opinion, what makes people happier: love or money? Why?
3. Who is the happiest person you know? Why?
4. How do you celebrate birthdays in your country?
5. Have you ever been very lucky (or unlucky)? Explain.
6. Do you prefer movies with sad or happy endings? Why?
7. Are you proud of your country? Why or why not?
8. In your culture, how do you congratulate people on these occasions? What do you say?

   a. birth of a child
   b. marriage
   c. graduation from school
   d. promotion at work
   e. retirement from a job

Now change partners. Ask your new partner the same questions about his or her first partner. Use the third person, as in this example:

EXAMPLE: What "little things" make him or her feel happy?
[say] **A phone call from his friend...** } **makes him happy.**
A letter from home...

ONE STEP FURTHER

Choose a feeling from this chapter.

Draw a person with that feeling.

Now draw a  above the head of the person you drew.

Exchange your picture with your partner.

Your partner must write what the person is thinking in the .

Now exchange your picture again with your partner.

Talk about the pictures.

Ask about your partner's feelings.

▨▨▨▨ PROBLEM SOLVING

Read the situation and possible solutions.
Which is the best solution? Write 1 next to the best idea, 2 next to the
  second best idea, and so forth.
Then work in groups of three or four.
Choose a secretary for your group.
Discuss your answers. Decide as a group the best order of the solutions.
The group secretary may write down the numbers.
Compare the answers of the different groups in the class.
Discuss why you chose certain solutions.

SITUATION: After a serious accident one year ago, doctors told you that
you would never walk again. But after an operation and months of
physical therapy*, tomorrow you will be able to walk with a cane.

WHAT SHOULD YOU DO?

a. _____ Invite your family and friends to the hospital. Surprise them
          by walking alone for the first time. Have a party to celebrate
          your progress†.

b. _____ Have a party and congratulate yourself on your achievement.
          Explain proudly that you accomplished your goal yourself.
          Don't be grateful to anyone else for helping you.

c. _____ Have a party and make a toast to the people who helped you to
          recover. Praise your doctors and nurses for their encourage-
          ment. Relax and enjoy yourself at the party.

d. _____ Don't feel excited and lucky to walk again and don't celebrate
          your improvement. Feel sorry for yourself because you were in
          an accident and had to learn to walk again.

e. _____ Share your enthusiasm with the public by writing a book
          about your experience. Encourage other accident victims to
          reach their goals.

f. _____ (your own solution)_____

_____

_____

---

*therapy (n.) = treatment by exercise, heat, and so forth
†progress (n.) = improvement

▨▨▨▨ WORDPLAY

A. **Prepositions.** Complete the story with the correct prepositions. Use *about, of, on, for, with,* or *to.*

Today was an exciting day at the Rising Sun Market! June Chung, a cashier at this small grocery store, won $10,000 in the state lottery. After the announcement, June told me that she was very **surprised** __about__ winning and very **pleased** _____ her
1   2
accomplishment.

June's parents own this small market. They are, of course, especially **happy** _____ their daughter. All their friends and
3
customers are **congratulating** her _____ her fantastic
4
luck. The whole neighborhood is very **proud** _____ her.
5
Right now, they are all celebrating at a restaurant. Everyone is **excited** _____ June's good luck!
6

REPORTER: June, how do you feel right now?

JUNE: I feel very **lucky** _____ win and very
7
enthusiastic _____ spending the money!
8

REPORTER: Will you quit your job?

JUNE: Yes. I certainly will! I'm planning to use the money to study computers!

REPORTER: Good luck, June! And that's all for tonight. . . from the DBC News Network.

B. **Sentence Completion.** Make sentences from these words. Add prepositions and other words you need. Use the past or past continuous tense,
as appropriate.

EXAMPLE: June / be / happy / win / lottery

    [write]   June was happy about winning
            the lottery.

---

1. June / parents / be / proud / her

2. June / be / surprised / win

3. friends and customers / congratulate / June / her good luck

4. everyone / celebrate / June

5. June / be / enthusiastic / spend / the money

6. everyone / have / good time / party

C. **Parts of Speech.** Complete the story. Use the correct forms of the
words.

The people of San Marcos, a small town in New Mexico, are enthusiastic
about attending the wedding of Clara Moreno and Pedro Flores.

---

happiness = noun   **happy** = adjective   **happily** = adverb

---

1. Clara and Pedro are very ___happy___. They love each
other very much.

2. It is an important day for both of them. They are smiling
_____ at all the wedding guests.

3. Clara looks quietly at Pedro. She sees the _____ in
his eyes.

---

pride = noun   **proud** = adjective   **proudly** = adverb

---

4. Clara's parents smile with _____ at their lucky daughter.

5. Pedro's parents are also very _____ of their son.

6. After the ceremony, Pedro _____ holds the hand of his new wife.

---

luck = noun   **lucky** = adjective   **luckily** = adverb

---

7. Clara's family thinks she is very _____ to marry Pedro.

8. It is difficult to find a good job in San Marcos. But _____, both Pedro and Clara can work on the Flores ranch.

9. All the people of the town wish the happy young couple good _____.

---

joy = noun   **enjoy** = verb   **joyfully** = adverb

---

10. Finally, with tears in her eyes, Mrs. Flores says, "This wedding gives us all a lot of _____."

11. "Now, everyone is invited to _____ a delicious barbecue at the ranch!"

12. After the celebration, the young couple hugs everyone _____ and leaves for their honeymoon.

DISCUSSION (optional)

1. Describe a wedding celebration in your culture. What does the couple wear?

2. At what age do most men and women marry in your culture?

3. Does the couple usually go on a honeymoon after the ceremony?

4. Is everyone always happy at weddings? Does anyone ever cry? Why?

C H A P T E R 2
❁ SADNESS

- ❁ EXPRESSING LONELINESS
- ❁ CONSOLING SOMEONE
- ❁ TELLING BAD NEWS
- ❁ REACTING TO BAD NEWS
- ❁ EXPRESSING GRIEF
- ❁ ACCEPTING SYMPATHY

▨▨▨▨ HARD TIMES

Look at the pictures and vocabulary words. Talk about what is happening in each picture.

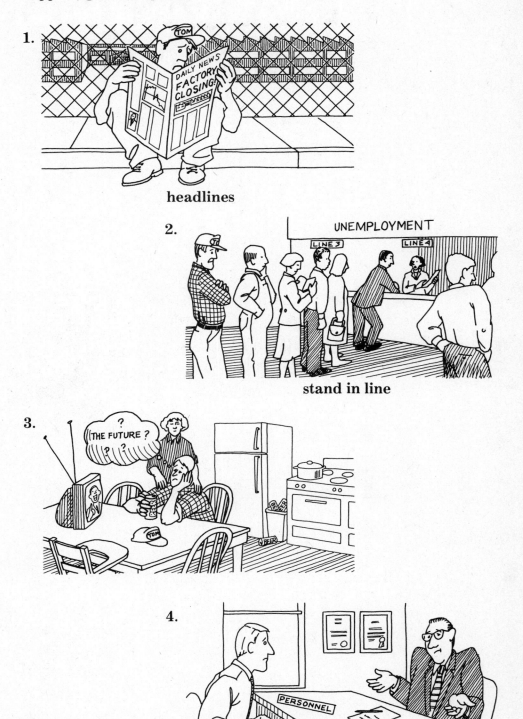

1.

headlines

2.

stand in line

3.

job interview

4.

5.

bad news

6.

get drunk

7.

8.

death / pray

▨▨▨▨ WORDS AND EXPRESSIONS

expression	example
be bored with { + VERB*ing* / someone or something } (= not be interested)	I'm bored with { studying history. / my history teacher. }
be in a rut (= be in an unchanging situation)	She's in a rut. She really needs a vacation.
be { **sad** / **unhappy** / **depressed** } **about** { + VERB*ing* / something } (= feel bad about)	He's { unhappy about changing his schedule at work. / sad about the news. / depressed about his mother's death. }
be in a bad mood about something (= feel negative, usually for a short time)	Chris was in a bad mood when I called her; she didn't feel like talking.
be down (in the dumps) *(slang)* (= feel depressed)	Don't bother him; he's been down (in the dumps) for days.
be in / **get into** } **trouble** (= have a problem)	She { was in / got into } trouble with her teacher about her grades.
be { **unlucky** / **unfortunate** } (= have bad things happen)	He was unlucky in love. It is unfortunate that you lost your wallet.
be a { **bummer** *(slang)* / **drag** *(slang)* } (= be unfortunate)	What a { bummer! / drag! } I got a parking ticket.
be sorry about { + VERB*ing* / something } (= feel bad about something that happened)	I am sorry about { forgetting our appointment. / your husband's illess. }
feel sorry for someone (= feel bad because of another person's situation)	I feel sorry for people without homes.
regret { + VERB*ing* / something } (= feel bad about something that happened in the past)	After a year alone, he regrets { getting a divorce. / his decision. }
disappoint someone **let** someone **down** (= not do what someone expects you to do)	You { disappointed me / let me down } when you didn't call.
be disappointed { **about** { + VERB*ing* / something } / **in** someone } (= be unhappy because something happens that you don't like)	We're disappointed about { losing the game. / the low salary. } I'm disappointed in you because you never write me.

expression	example
be discouraged $\left\{ \begin{array}{l} \textbf{about} \\ \textbf{by} \end{array} \right\}$ something (= want to give up because of difficulties)	I am discouraged $\left\{ \begin{array}{l} about \\ by \end{array} \right\}$ my grades.
be worried about $\left\{ \begin{array}{l} \text{+ VERB}ing \\ \text{something} \end{array} \right.$ (= feel uneasy)	She's worried about $\left\{ \begin{array}{l} missing\ the\ plane. \\ the\ exam. \end{array} \right.$
be $\left\{ \begin{array}{l} \textbf{frustrated about} \text{ a situation} \\ \textbf{fed up with} \text{ someone or something} \end{array} \right.$ (= be annoyed or irritated)	I'm frustrated about the parking problem here. He's fed up with his roommate.
be pessimistic about something (= expect the worst to happen; opposite of *optimistic*)	He is pessimistic about the situation.
be **feel** $\left. \begin{array}{l} \\ \end{array} \right\}$ **lonely** (= be unhappy because you are without company or because family and friends are far away)	Sometimes I $\left\{ \begin{array}{l} am \\ feel \end{array} \right\}$ lonely because I live by myself.
miss someone or something (= feel unhappy because someone or something is not nearby)	When I miss my sister, I usually call her. Now that I have a new car, I miss my old car.
be homesick (= miss your family or country when you are away)	The movie about my country made me homesick.
be desperate to + VERB something (= be ready to do anything to get what you want)	The woman was desperate to feed her hungry children, so she stole the food.
be hopeless (= feel that what is wanted will not happen)	The situation is hopeless; there is no solution.
commit suicide (= kill oneself)	Thousands of depressed people commit suicide each year.

❖❖❖❖ TELLING THE STORY

Look at the picture story to answer these questions. Pay special
attention to the words **in dark type**.

1. Why is Tom **unhappy about** the headline?

2. What are the workers in line at the unemployment office
   depressed about?

3. Why is Tom **in a bad mood** at home? How does his wife act?

4. Is Tom optimistic or **pessimistic about** getting a new job? Why
   does he feel **discouraged** at the interview?

5. Why does he feel **disappointed about** the phone call?

6. When Tom starts to think his situation is **hopeless**, how does he act at home?

7. Tom's wife becomes **desperate** because of his behavior. What does she do?

8. When Tom finally **regrets** his actions, what does he think about?

9. How do you know he is **sorry about** what he did?

⊞⊞⊞⊞ FINISHING THE STORY

1. What will Tom decide in church?

2. How will he feel after that?

3. What will he do next?

⊞⊞⊞⊞ BODY LANGUAGE

A. Match each picture with a description of the action. Write the correct letter on the line.

A.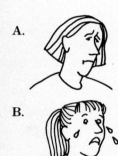

B.

C.

1. _____ frown (at)

2. _____ put one's head in one's hands

3. _____ put one's hand on someone's shoulder

4. _____ hold / hug

5. _____ cry / weep / sob

B. Work in pairs. Cover the words. Look only at the pictures. Describe what each person is doing and why. (Make up your explanations.)

EXAMPLE: Picture A
  1. What's she doing?   She's frowning
  2. Why?   . . . because she's sad.
            . . . because her friend didn't call.

C. In groups, talk about cultural differences. Answer these questions:

1. Do people in your culture show their feelings of sadness in the same way as in the pictures?

2. Do men in your culture show sadness in the same way as women? Is it acceptable for men to cry in public?

3. In what other ways do you express sadness?

Summarize your discussion for the class.

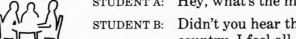 # EXPRESSIONS AND CONVERSATIONS

A. Practice the following conversation with your partner. Use the appropriate body language to act out (dramatize) the situation.

STUDENT A: Hey, what's the matter? You look depressed.

STUDENT B: Didn't you hear the news? My brother went back to our country. <u>I feel all alone</u> now.

STUDENT A: I understand <u>your situation</u>. But <u>don't let it bother you too much</u>. Remember, I'm here! You don't have to <u>feel lonely</u>.

STUDENT B: Yeah, you're right. But <u>I miss him</u>, anyway.

STUDENT A: Come on. <u>Cheer up! Everything will be all right</u>. You've got a friend.

B. Now practice the conversation again. Use different expressions for the underlined words. Have several different conversations.

EXAMPLE: [instead of] I feel all alone.
           [say] **I feel all by myself.**

▣ Expressing Loneliness   (= saying you feel unhappy because you are without company or far away from people you know)

I feel $\begin{cases} \text{lonely.} \\ \text{all alone.} \\ \text{all by myself.} \end{cases}$

I'm homesick.

I miss $\begin{cases} \text{my family.} \\ \text{my country.} \end{cases}$

▣ Consoling Someone   (= trying to make someone feel better)

I understand $\begin{cases} \text{your situation.} \\ \text{your problem.} \end{cases}$

I know $\begin{cases} \text{what you mean.} \\ \text{how you feel.} \\ \text{how it is.} \end{cases}$

Don't let it $\begin{cases} \text{bother you too much.} \\ \text{get you down.} \end{cases}$

Cheer up!
Don't feel bad!

Everything will be all right.
Things will get better.

C. Practice the following conversation with your partner.

DOCTOR: <u>I'm sorry to tell you this</u>, but your son has been seriously hurt in an accident.

PARENT: Oh, no! <u>I can't believe it</u>! <u>How terrible</u>!

DOCTOR: Well, <u>I'm afraid</u> it's true. We have to operate on him immediately.

PARENT: Oh, no! <u>It isn't possible</u>! He was fine this morning.

Practice the conversation again. Use expressions from the following list instead of the underlined words.

▨ Telling Bad News

I'm sorry to tell you this, but...
I hate to say this, but...

I'm afraid that...
Unfortunately,...

▨ Reacting to Bad News

I can't believe it!   **How terrible!**
I don't believe it!   **How awful!**
It's hard to believe!

It { **can't be true!**
    { **isn't possible!**

D. Practice the following conversation with your partner.

WOMAN A: I received your card yesterday. <u>Thank you for your sympathy</u>.

WOMAN B: <u>I'm so sorry</u>. Your grandfather was such a wonderful person. I'll miss him.

WOMAN A: <u>That's very kind of you</u>. Of course, we'll all miss him!

WOMAN B: <u>I can't tell you how sad I am</u>. Is there anything I can do to help?

Practice the conversation again. Use expressions from the following list instead of the underlined words.

✦ Expressing Grief   (*grief* = a feeling of deep sadness)

I'm so sorry.
It's such a shame.

I can't tell you how sad I am!
You have no idea how terrible I feel!

✦ Accepting Sympathy   (*sympathy* = understanding another person's grief)

Thank you for your sympathy.
I really appreciate your concern.

That's very $\begin{cases} \text{kind} \\ \text{nice} \\ \text{thoughtful} \end{cases}$ of you.

E. Now role play the situations in this section. Use your own words and the appropriate body language. How do you feel in each situation?

⊞⊞⊞⊞ EXPRESSING YOURSELF

A. **How Do They Feel?** Find a partner. Ask and answer questions about the story at the beginning of the chapter. Use *feel, look,* or *act.*

EXAMPLE: **Picture 1**
1. **How does (Tom) look? He looks unhappy.**
2. **Why? ...because the plant is closing and he's losing his job.**

B. **How Would You Feel?** Work with your partner. Take turns asking and answering the following questions. Use the correct preposition.

SITUATION: You have just lost your job.

EXAMPLE: What are you sad _____? *(losing my job)*
What are you sad about? I'm sad about losing my job.

---

1. What are you unhappy _____? *(my money situation)*

2. What were you depressed _____? *(the long hours and low pay)*

3. What are you discouraged _____ now? *(not having another job)*

4. Why are you so down _____ the dumps?* *(nobody wants to hire me)*

5. What are you desperate _____ do? *(find a new job)*

6. Why are you _____ a bad mood?* *(I need another job and I can't find one)*

---

*Remember: Use *because (of)* to answer a question with *why.*

▓▓▓▓ ROLE PLAY

Work with a partner.
Choose one of the following situations.
Each student plays one role.
Read and think only about your role.
How do you feel?
Act out the situations. Use expressions from this chapter.
(Your teacher may ask a third student to direct and give suggestions.)

Role A	Role B
1. It is your first week in a new country. You feel very lonely and homesick. You miss your family and friends. You try to explain to your classmate how you feel.	1. You are the classmate. You understand your new friend's feelings because you have felt the same way before. You try to make him or her feel at home.
2. You're very depressed. You are usually a good student, but you were busy and couldn't study for the final exam. You failed and now you want to re-take it. You explain to your teacher why you didn't study for the exam.	2. You are the teacher. You are very disappointed because your student failed the exam. Unfortunately, you must follow school rules. You tell the student that he or she must take the entire course again.
3. Your oldest child is going away to college and you will miss him or her. You are at the beauty or barber shop complaining about this to the person who is cutting your hair.	3. You are the beautician or barber. You have older children, and you understand how your customer feels. You describe your feelings when your children left home.
4. Your grandfather has just died at the age of 85. The phone rings. You talk about your feelings to your friend.	4. You find out that your friend's grandfather has just died, and you call to console him or her.
5. You are a police officer. You have just arrested the son of a famous politican for selling drugs. You have to call the parents to tell them the bad news.	5. You are the surprised parent. You can't believe your child is in trouble. You didn't even know he used drugs.
6. (your own situation) ?	6. (your own situation) ?

⊠⊠⊠⊠ INTERVIEW

Ask your partner the following questions. Take notes on the answers. (Your teacher may ask you to do this exercise in groups of three or four.)

1. In what situations do you feel sad? Give three examples.

_____

EXAMPLE: [say] **I feel sad when I think about my country.**

_____

2. People say, "Without sadness, you cannot appreciate happiness." Do you agree? Do people say something similar in your language?

3. How do you usually act when you are in a bad mood? How do the people around you *re*act?

4. Is it healthy to act happy when you really feel depressed? If someone is depressed for a long time, what should he or she do?

5. Have you ever been disappointed in someone or something? Describe your experience.

6. Do you ever feel lonely? When you miss someone, or feel homesick, what makes you feel better?

7. What do you think is the best way to cheer up a sad friend?

8. Should news photographers take pictures of people (famous or not) in very sad, personal situations? Why or why not?

Now change partners. Ask your new partner the same questions about his or her first partner. Use the third person, as in this example:

_____

EXAMPLE: In what situations does she feel sad?
            [say] **She feels sad when she thinks about her country.**

_____

⊠⊠⊠⊠ ONE STEP FURTHER

Choose a feeling from this chapter.

Draw a person with that feeling on this page.

Now draw a ⟨cloud⟩ above the head of the person you drew.

Exchange your picture with your partner.

Your partner must draw what the person is thinking in the ⟨cloud⟩.

Now exchange your picture again with your partner.

Talk about the pictures.

Ask about your partner's feelings.

▣▣▣▣ PROBLEM SOLVING

Read the situation and possible solutions to yourself.
Which is the best solution? Write 1 next to the best idea, 2 next to the
    second best idea, and so forth.
Then work in groups of three or four.
Choose a secretary for your group.
Discuss your answers. Decide as a group the best order of the solutions.
The group secretary may write down the numbers.
Compare the answers of the different groups in the class.
Discuss why you chose certain solutions.

SITUATION: You meet someone, fall in love, and decide to get married.
The week before the wedding, your fiance* changes his or her mind
and breaks the engagement†.

WHAT SHOULD YOU DO?

a. _____ Blame yourself for his or her "change of heart." Become very
            depressed and spend weeks alone. Regret everything you said
            and did.

b. _____ Feel sorry for yourself. Decide never to get engaged again.
            Don't accept any dates for a year.

c. _____ Try to get over your sorrow and disappointment. Go out,
            dance, and try to have a good time. Look for someone else.

d. _____ Write an honest letter to your ex-fiance. Tell him or her that
            your feelings are very hurt. Then try to forget and start life
            again.

e. _____ Call your ex-fiance every night, cry, and ask him or her to
            come back. Hope that your ex-fiance will change his or her
            mind again.

f. _____ Pretend that you don't care at all about what happened. Meet
            and start dating someone else immediately.

g. _____ (your own solution)_____

_____

_____

_____

*fiance (n.) = person you plan to marry.
†engagement (n.) = agreement to marry.

✖✖✖✖ WORDPLAY

A. **Prepositions.** Complete the story with the correct prepositions. Use *about, with, in, to, down,* or *for.*

I don't know what to do, Dr. Tanaka. I just feel **sad** <u>about</u>
_____
                                                                          1
everything in my life. After I lost my job at the plant, I got very

depressed _____ the future. I guess I was **feeling sorry**
                                2

_____ myself. I was _____ **a bad mood**
          3   4
all the time.

One day, I had a job interview at another factory. I was pretty

pessimistic _____ it because I'm forty-eight years old.
                        5
Well, the next day when I found out that I didn't get the job, I realized

that my wife, Nancy, was **disappointed** _____ me.
                                                             6

Then I got more **frustrated** _____ my situation. I
                                             7
started drinking too much and yelling at Nancy. I realize now that

I **let** her _____ . Finally, she got **fed up** _____
                  8   9
me and left with the kids. After that, I really became **desperate**

_____ end everything. I wanted to die, but I prayed for
          10
help instead. Then, I decided to talk to a counselor.* That's why I'm

here. I hope you can help me.

B. **Sentence Completion.** Make sentences from these words. Add
prepositions and other words you need. Use the past tense.

_____

EXAMPLE: why / be / Tom / unhappy / headline?

      [write]   Why was Tom unhappy about
                    the headline ?

_____

_____
*counselor (n.) = person who talks to people about their problems

1. he / be / worried / future

_____

2. after / they / lose / their jobs, / workers / be / depressed

_____

3. when / Tom / be / bad mood / he / drink / too much

_____

4. why / be / Tom / pessimistic / interview?

_____

5. after / interview / he / be / disappointed / because / he / do / not get / job

_____

6. Tom / be / frustrated / because / he / can't / find / job

_____

7. wife / leave / him / because / he / drink / too much / and / yell / her

_____

8. after / wife / leave / him, / he / feel / sorry / yell / her

_____

C. **Parts of Speech**. Complete the story. Use the correct forms of the words.

This morning, the people of Altamira are attending the funeral* of kind old Señora† Ramos. For many years, she was a popular teacher in the village school.

*funeral (n.) = ceremony to bury a dead person
† señora = Spanish for "Mrs." or "lady"

---

death = noun   **dead** = adjective   **die** = verb

---

1. "Is Señora Ramos really ____dead____?" the children ask their parents.

2. "Yes, she _____ last night in her sleep," the parents reply.

3. "But she was very old. Her _____ was not a surprise," they explain softly.

---

pain = noun (opposite   **painful** = adjective   **hurt** = verb (cause pain)
of pleasure)

---

4. The news of her death is very _____ for the children.

5. They all loved the old woman. "How can she leave us? It _____ us so much," they whisper.

6. The parents can see the _____ in the children's eyes.

---

sadness = noun   **sad** = adjective   **sadly** = adverb

---

7. The funeral is a very _____ occasion.

8. The men and women of the village wear traditional black clothes to show their _____ .

9. The church bells ring _____ .

---

tears = noun   **cry** = verb   **tearfully** = adverb

---

10. The older children _____. They understand the meaning of death.

11. But the younger children ask _____, "Where is Señora Ramos?"

12. "She is far away," the older ones explain with _____ in their eyes. "She will never come back."

DISCUSSION (optional)

1. Are funerals always very sad, serious occasions in your culture?

2. What color clothing do family and friends wear to funerals in your culture? For how long do they wear this color?

3. What do you say to express sympathy in your culture when someone dies?

4. In your religion, what is the attitude toward death? Is there a belief in life after death?

CHAPTER 3

HUMOR

▦▦▦▦ THE UNINVITED GUEST*

Look at the pictures and vocabulary words. Talk about what is happening in each picture.

1. ANNUAL BARBECUE
   WHO INVITED THEM?

   barbecue

2. DID YOU HEAR THE JOKE ABOUT THE WET TEXAN?

   Texan

3. TEE-HEE!

   shoot / squirt gun

4. YOU MISSED!

   Frisbee

5.

idea

6.

hot pepper / bowl of chili†

7.

8.

---

*uninvited guest = person who no one invited to a party or other event
†chili = meat and bean dish

▦▦▦▦ WORDS AND EXPRESSIONS

expression	example
have a (good) sense of humor (= see what is funny in any situation)	*My friend has a good sense of humor; she laughs about her problems.*
be { **funny** **humorous** **amusing** **entertaining** } (= make people laugh)	*He's a* { *funny* *humorous* } *teacher. He makes us laugh.* *That movie was* { *amusing.* *entertaining.* } *It made me laugh.*
be hilarious (= make people laugh very hard)	*The clowns in the circus are hilarious.*
crack someone **up** *(slang)* (= make someone laugh)	*That joke really cracks me up.*
be a riot *(slang)* (= be very funny)	*Your roommate is a riot.*
be { **silly** **ridiculous** } (= be a. childish b. without common sense)	*a. You look silly with that basket on your head.* *b. It's ridiculous to wear a sweater in this heat.*
make a sarcastic remark (= say the opposite of what you feel)	*He made a sarcastic remark: "Oh, yeah, the movie was great! I left after ten minutes."*
joke **kid** **(around) with** } someone { + VERB*ing* **about** something (= not be serious)	*The coach* { *joked (around) with* *kidded* } *the team about* { *losing the game.* *the score.* }
put someone **on** *(slang)* (= joke with someone)	*You're putting me on. You're not really from New York; you're from Chicago.*
tell a joke (jokes) about something **to** someone (= tell a funny story)	*She told a joke about an elephant to the class.*
tell { **a dirty** **an off-color** } **joke to** someone (= tell a story about sex or the human body)	*Nobody at the party laughed at his* { *dirty* *off-color* } *jokes.*
play a joke on someone (= do something to someone to make other people laugh)	*Students sometimes play jokes on their teachers.*
make fun of someone (= do or say something funny that hurts someone's feelings)	*They made fun of me because I didn't know how to play the game.*
put someone **down** *(slang)* (= make fun of someone)	*They put him down because of his accent.*

expression	example
embarrass someone **by** + VERB*ing* something (= cause someone to feel uncomfortable)	*He embarrassed her by telling dirty jokes.*
insult **offend** } someone (= say or do something rude or unkind)	*The guest's comments about the food* { *offended / insulted* } *the cook.*
get even with someone **pay** someone **back for** something (= do something funny or mean to someone who has done something unkind)	*I'll* { *get even with you / pay you back* } *for that remark.*

▨▨▨▨ TELLING THE STORY

Look at the picture story to answer these questions. Pay special attention to the words **in dark type**.

1. Is the woman smiling at the uninvited guest when he arrives? Does she think he is **amusing**?
2. What does the uninvited guest **tell a joke** about?
3. Why does he shoot the squirt gun? Who is he **making fun of**?
4. Does the Texan think the joke is **funny**? Why or why not?
5. When does the Texan decide to **get even with** the guest?
6. What kind of **joke** does the Texan **play on** him?
7. After he eats the bowl of chili, does the guest still want to **joke around with** the other guests? Why or why not?
8. At the end of the story, does the guest still **have a sense of humor**?

▨▨▨▨ FINISHING THE STORY

1. Where is the first place the guest will stop?
2. Will he ever eat chili again?
3. Will his girlfriend leave him? Why or why not?

▓▓▓▓ BODY LANGUAGE

A. Match each picture with a description of the action(s). Write the correct letter on the line.

1. _____ grin (at), smile (at, about)

2. _____ wink (at)

3. _____ make a face (at)

4. _____ giggle (at, about)

5. _____ laugh (at, about)

B. Work in pairs. Cover the words. Look only at the pictures. Describe what each person is doing and why. (Make up your explanations.)

EXAMPLE: **Picture C**
  1. **What's she doing?**   She's grinning.
  2. **Why?**   . . .because someone is making a face at her
       . . .because someone is telling a funny story.

C. In groups, talk about cultural differences. Answer these questions:

1. When they hear or see something funny, do people in your culture show amusement the same way as in the pictures?

2. Do men in your culture express humor in the same way as women? What about children?

3. In what other ways do you express humor or amusement?

Summarize your discussion for the class.

▨▨▨▨ EXPRESSIONS AND CONVERSATIONS

A. Practice the following conversation with your partner. Use the appropriate body language to act out (dramatize) the situation.

HUSBAND: Oh my gosh, I just won $50,000 in the lottery!

WIFE: <u>Be serious.</u> $50,000? I can't believe it!...Come on, you didn't win anything! <u>Don't tease me!</u>

HUSBAND: It's true! <u>I'm not kidding!</u>...*(starts laughing)* All right, how did you guess <u>I'm just joking</u>?

WIFE: Oh, I can tell! From now on, <u>stop kidding around</u>! Do you want me to have a heart attack?

B. Now practice the conversation again. Use different expressions for the underlined words. Have several different conversations.

EXAMPLE: [instead of] I'm serious!
           [say] **I'm not kidding!**

▨ **Teasing** (= annoying someone by making fun of him or her)

I'm serious!	*or*	I'm not serious!
I'm (just) kidding!		I'm not kidding!
I'm joking!		I'm not joking!

▨ **Reacting to Teasing**

Don't tease me!	Stop teasing me!
Don't joke with me!	Stop { kidding / joking } around!
Don't kid me!	

Be serious!
Get serious!

C. Practice the following conversation with your partner.

A: Hey, <u>have you heard the joke</u> about the couple who . . .

B: Oh, please, not another dirty joke! <u>Why don't you tell</u> a clean joke for a change!

A: What a minute! <u>This is the funniest joke I've ever told!</u>

B: Listen, I don't care! <u>I'd prefer to hear</u> a clean joke this time, if you don't mind!

Practice the conversation again. Use expressions from the following list instead of the underlined words.

▣ Telling Jokes

Have you heard the joke about the elephant?
Did you hear the story about the airplane?

This is the best joke I've ever heard!
This is the funniest joke in the world!

▣ Talking about Jokes

I'd like to hear the joke about the elephant.
Why don't you tell the one about the monkey?

I'd rather hear the joke about the librarian.
I'd prefer to hear the one about the mechanic.

D. Practice the following conversation with your partner.

PARENT: Did you <u>have fun</u> at the movies with your brother?

CHILD: Oh yeah, Mom, it was great! The movie <u>was really funny</u>!

PARENT: <u>Was</u> your little brother <u>good</u>? Tell me the truth!

CHILD: Well, no, not really. He <u>was acting silly</u> during the first half of the movie.

Practice the conversation again. Use expressions from the following list instead of the underlined words.

❖ Describing the Behavior of Children

Was he **good?**   He **was acting silly.**
Did he **behave** himself?   She **was acting like a baby.**

❖ Talking about Enjoyable Experiences

Did you $\begin{cases} \textbf{have fun*?} \\ \textbf{have a good time?} \\ \textbf{enjoy yourselves?} \end{cases}$ The movie **was really funny.**
      The show **made me laugh.**

E. Now role play the situations in this section. Use your own words and the appropriate body language. How do you feel in each situation?

---

*fun (n.) = enjoyment; funny (adj.) = amusing

▨▨▨▨ EXPRESSING YOURSELF

What Do You Say? Use these expressions in your answers to the questions that follow.

EXPRESSIONS

She cracks me up.   I'm just kidding.

I'm insulted.   How embarrassing!

That's ridiculous.   Don't be silly.

Are you being sarcastic?

You're putting me on...   It's $\begin{cases} \text{a riot!} \\ \text{hilarious!} \end{cases}$

EXAMPLE: What do you say when you're not being serious?
        [say] **I'm just kidding.**

WHAT DO YOU SAY?

1. ...when you're recommending a funny movie to a friend?

2. ...when someone tells you a funny but unbelievable story?

3. ...when someone says $50 is a cheap price for a meal in a restaurant?

4. ...when you're watching a very funny actress on your favorite TV program?

5. ...when someone tells you a joke about people of your nationality?

6. ...when a parking lot attendant tells you that you owe $20 for one hour?

7. ...when a friend will not accept an expensive present from you?

8. ...when you go out with your friends and someone drinks too much and tells dirty jokes at the dinner table?

▨▨▨▨ ROLE PLAY

Work with a partner.
Choose one of the following situations.
Each student plays one role.
Read and think only about your role.
How do you feel?
Act out the situations. Use expressions from this chapter.
(Your teacher may ask a third student to direct and give suggestions.)

Role A	Role B
1. You love to play jokes on your roommate, even though you know he or she doesn't like it. You leave a large plastic spider in his or her coffee cup. You start giggling and laughing while you watch.	1. You are the roommate, and you are tired of your friend's jokes. After you scream about the spider, you explain that his or her jokes are not funny any more. You complain that this is the third time you have asked him or her to stop playing jokes.
2. You are an office manager and don't have a very good sense of humor. You didn't sleep well last night and fall asleep at your desk while reading the newspaper. When you wake up, you're not laughing.	2. You notice your boss sleeping at his or her desk and you start grinning. You tell the other workers to come over to look at the boss. Everyone giggles and makes faces. When he or she suddenly wakes up, you are all very embarrassed.
3. You speak English but your accent is difficult to understand. When you order "flench flies" at a restaurant, it sounds like you are joking and don't really want anything. But you are hungry, and repeat your order several times.	3. You are a waiter or waitress. When the customer orders "flench flies," you start giggling. Is he or she serious or kidding? You are not sure, but you think his or her accent is very funny and cute. You joke around with the customer.
4. Your friend is trying to learn how to dance. You are already a good dancer. Instead of helping, you giggle, laugh and imitate his or her mistakes.	4. You are learning to dance. When your friend makes fun of you, you decide to get even with him or her. You have a new record with you, but refuse to play it until he or she apologizes!
5. (your own situation) ?	5. (your own situation) ?

▨▨▨▨ INTERVIEW

Ask your partner the following questions. Take notes on the answers. (Your teacher may ask you to do this exercise in groups of three or four.)

1. Are you basically a serious or a funny person?

_____

EXAMPLE: [say] **I think that I'm a funny person because I like to make people laugh.**

_____

2. Do you ever tell jokes? Why or why not?

3. Do you like funny movies (comedies)? Who is your favorite funny actor or actress (comedian)? Why is he or she funny?

4. Do you think a sense of humor is important in life? In relationships with other people? Why?

5. Do you laugh at jokes about other nationalities or races? What about dirty jokes? Why or why not?

6. Do some jokes embarrass you? If someone tells a joke that offends you, what do you do?

7. If you don't understand a joke in English, how do you react?

8. Is it normal for children to make fun of other children? How do you explain to a child why he or she shouldn't make fun of another person?

Now change partners. Ask your new partner the same questions about his or her first partner. Use the third person, as in this example:

_____

EXAMPLE: Is he a serious or a funny person?
      [say] **He's a funny person because he likes to make people laugh.**

_____

▨▨▨▨ ONE STEP FURTHER

GAME: "LANGUAGE AND LAUGHTER"

For this game you will need 3″ x 5″ cards.

1. Work with a group of students (or a partner). If possible, work with people who speak your native language.

2. Talk about jokes (or funny stories) that you know. (You can use your native language if everyone in the group understands it.)

3. Work together. Try to tell a simple joke (or funny story) _from your culture_ in English. (If everyone in the group speaks the same

language, translate two jokes; if students speak different languages, each person tells a joke.)

4. Write the jokes in English on the card.

5. After the teacher collects the cards, he or she will read the jokes one by one.

6. After each joke, the students must try to guess the original language of the joke. (If it is your joke, don't say anything.)

7. How many jokes are there from each culture? Keep a record on the board.

8. Which joke is the funniest?

▣▣▣▣ PROBLEM SOLVING

Read the situation and possible solutions to yourself.
Which is the best solution? Write 1 next to the best idea, 2 next to the second best idea, and so forth.
Then work in groups of three or four.
Choose a secretary for your group.
Discuss your answers. Decide as a group the best order of the solutions.
The group secretary may write down the numbers.
Compare the answers of the different groups in the class.
Discuss why you chose certain solutions.

SITUATION: It's your first month at a new job. You like your job, but you feel uncomfortable there. The manager is not from your culture, and sometimes he makes fun of your accent. He occasionally makes unkind jokes about other cultures, as well.

WHAT SHOULD YOU DO?

a. _____ Tell the manager that you don't like his sense of humor. Quit your job.

b. _____ Start to make loud jokes about the manager's culture.

c. _____ Don't pay attention to the manager. Do a good job and ignore him.

d. _____ Politely explain to the manager that he is offending you. Ask him to stop.

e. _____ Hire a lawyer and sue the manager for discrimination.

f. _____ Write a formal letter of complaint to the owner of the company. Ask him or her to speak to the manager about the problem.

g. _____ (your own solution)_____

_____

_____

❈❈❈❈ WORDPLAY

A. **Prepositions.** Complete the story with the correct prepositions. Use *by, on, about, back, at, down,* or *of.*

Nobody invited him. He just came to the barbecue without an invitation. And believe me, he was the loudest guy I've ever heard! Then, to make things worse, he started **telling jokes** ____about____ Texans. Next he **made fun** _____ 2 cowboys by shooting a toy squirt gun. Well, his girlfriend was **giggling** _____ 3 that, but nobody else was **laughing** _____ 4 his jokes. In fact, he **embarrassed** everyone at the party _____ 5 telling his stupid, boring stories!

Then I saw my neighbor, Tex, staring at him. "Good!" I thought. "Now maybe he'll learn a lesson about **putting** other people _____ 6 !" Nobody at the barbecue could stand him or his jokes anyway. Even the kids were **making faces** _____ 7 him during the Frisbee game. Then, Tex decided to **pay him** _____ 8 by putting hot pepper in his bowl of chili. Boy, did he **play a joke** _____ 9 him! But I think he really deserved it.

B. **Sentence Completion.** Make sentences from these words. Add prepositions and other words you need. Use the past or past continuous tense, as appropriate.

_____

EXAMPLE: why / women / not smile / uninvited guest / ?
[write] Why wasn't the woman smiling at the uninvited guest?

_____

1. when / he / tell / joke / Texans, / nobody / laugh

_____

2. he / make / fun / cowboys / with / his squirt gun

_____

3. Texan / do / not think / that / his jokes / be / funny

_____

4. children / make / faces / him / during / Frisbee game

_____

5. Texan / play / joke / him / with / hot pepper

_____

6. why / do / everybody / laugh / when / he / eat / chili / ?

_____

7. he / offend / Texan, / so / Texan / get even / him

_____

C. **Parts of Speech**. Complete the story. Use the correct forms of the words.

Every year, millions of tourists travel to the casinos of Las Vegas, Nevada, to gamble.* Gambling is not the only attraction in Las Vegas, however.

_____

entertainment = noun   **entertaining** = adjective   **entertain** = verb

_____

1. During the day, most visitors to Las Vegas <u>entertain</u> themselves in the casinos.

2. At night, many visitors are tired of gambling. They are looking for other kinds of _____ .

3. These tourists go to exciting and _____ nightclub shows.

_____

comedy = noun   **comedian** = noun (person)   **comic** = adjective

_____

4. There they see beautiful dancers and hear famous _____.

5. In Las Vegas _____ is a big business!

6. In fact, Las Vegas is famous for its _____ entertainment.

_____
*gamble (v.) = play cards (or other games) for money

---
sense of humor = noun   **humorous** = adjective   **humorously** = adverb

---

7. Many of the comedians in Las Vegas are very _____ .

8. They perform very _____ for their audiences.

9. But you need a special _____ to enjoy some of the comedians there.

---
embarrassment = noun   **embarrassing** = adjective   **embarrass** = verb

---

10. Some of their jokes are very _____ .

11. In fact, sometimes their stories _____ their audiences.

12. But most tourists get over their _____ and enjoy the shows anyway.

DISCUSSION (optional)

1. Why do you think people like to gamble?

2. Is gambling legal (allowed by law) or illegal (against the law) in your country?

3. In your opinion, is gambling wrong? Why or why not?

4. Do you think gambling should be legal everywhere? Why or why not?

5. Do you consider a lottery a form of gambling?

CHAPTER 4

ANGER

- COMPLAINING

- REFUSING

- GIVING ORDERS

- DISAGREEING

- AGREEING

- BLAMING SOMEONE FOR SOMETHING

- APOLOGIZING

▨▨▨▨ BAD DAY AT THE BANK

Look at the pictures and vocabulary words. Talk about what is
happening in each picture.

1.

manager / calendar

2.

clerk / doughnut

3.

secretaries / coffee machine

4.

customer / teller / make a mistake

5.

computer

6.

wait in line / dial

7.

yell

8.

supervisor

▨▨▨▨ WORDS AND EXPRESSIONS

expression	example
be nervous about { + VERB*ing* / something } (= be worried, a little afraid or excited)	I'm nervous about { *starting my job.* / *the new boss.* }
be { **upset** / **uptight** (*slang*) } **about** something (= be nervous, angry, or worried)	Don't talk to him right now. He's really { *upset* / *uptight* } about the parking ticket that he just got.
bother **annoy** **irritate** } someone **upset** (= make someone feel very uncomfortable or unhappy)	Please turn down that loud music. It's bothering me.
be { **annoyed** / **irritated** } **with** someone **for** + VERB*ing* **about** something (= feel disturbed)	She's { *annoyed with her friend for losing her book.* / *irritated about the noise.* }
be fed up with someone or something (= be tired of)	He's fed up with the high prices at this market.
be { **mad** / **angry** / **furious** } **at** someone **for** + VERB*ing* **about** something (= be extremely annoyed and unhappy)	I'm { *mad at my friend for lying to me.* / *angry about my low grades.* / *furious about this parking ticket.* }
lose one's temper (=get very angry)	If someone isn't fair to him, he loses his temper.
have a bad temper (=get angry often)	Be careful! When he's in a bad mood, he has a bad temper.
blow up at someone **hit the ceiling** (*slang*) (= lose one's temper)	When he saw the bill for the cold soup, he { *blew up at the waitress.* / *hit the ceiling.* }
discuss* something **with** someone (= talk about a topic from several different points of view)	We discussed the solution to the problem with our teacher.
argue† **quarrel** } **with** someone **about** something	I had { *an argument* / *a quarrel* } with my boss about my schedule.
have an { **argument** / **quarrel** } (= disagree strongly)	I { *quarreled* / *argued* } with my girlfriend last night.

*discuss (v.) = talk (usually in a friendly way); discussion (n.) = conversation
† argue (v.) = talk in an unfriendly way, disagree; argument (n.) = disagreement

expression	example
complain to someone **about** something (= tell someone that something is wrong)	*She complained to the waiter about the cold soup.*
blame someone **for** something (= say that someone is responsible for something wrong)	*The police officer blamed me for the accident, but it wasn't my fault.*
be someone's **fault** (fault = responsibility)	*I broke the dish. It's my fault.*
apologize to someone **for** + VERB*ing* (= say that you are sorry)	*He apologized to her for spilling the soup.*

▨▨▨▨ TELLING THE STORY

Look at the picture story to answer these questions. Pay special attention to the words **in dark type.**

1. What is the manager **nervous about**?
2. Why does the manager get **annoyed with** the clerk?
3. Why does he get **upset with** the secretaries?
4. What is the customer **complaining about**?
5. What do the customer and the teller **argue about**?
6. Is the mistake the teller's **fault**? Whose **fault** is it?
7. Why does the teller **apologize to** the customer?
8. What are the customers in line **angry about**?
9. Why does the manager finally **lose** his **temper**?

▨▨▨▨ FINISHING THE STORY

1. What do you think will happen during the supervisor's visit?
2. Will the supervisor find out about all the problems at the bank?
3. Will the manager lose his job?

▣▣▣▣ BODY LANGUAGE

A. Match each picture with a description of the action(s). Write the correct letter on the line.

A.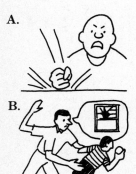

1. _____ stare (at)

2. _____ point (at)

3. _____ shake one's finger (at)

4. _____ bang one's fist (on the table)

5. _____ yell / shout / scream (at)

6. _____ spank

B.

B. Work in pairs. Cover the words. Look only at the pictures. Describe what each person is doing and why. (Make up your explanations.)

C.

D

EXAMPLE: Picture E
  1. What's she doing?   She's staring at someone.
  2. Why?   ...because she's angry at him.
         ...because he hit her car.

E.

C. In groups, talk about cultural differences. Answer these questions:

1. Do people in your culture show their feelings of anger in the same way as in the pictures?

2. Do men in your culture express anger in the same way as women?

F.

3. In your culture, what do parents do when they get angry at their children?

4. Do you think it is right to spank young children? Do parents in your culture sometimes spank their children?

Summarize your discussion for the class.

▓▓▓▓ EXPRESSIONS AND CONVERSATIONS

A. Practice the following conversation with your partner. Use the appropriate body language to act out (dramatize) the situation.

CHILD: No, I'm not going to eat this. I hate peas.

PARENT: Come on...you have to finish your peas. They're good for you.

CHILD: But I can't stand peas! They're terrible.

PARENT: Please, stop complaining and finish your peas. I'm sick and tired of your complaints, do you hear?

B. Now practice the conversation again. Use different expressions for the underlined words. Have several different conversations.

EXAMPLE: [instead of]   I'm not going to...
              [say]   **I refuse to...**

▓ **Complaining**   (= telling someone what you don't like or what is wrong)

I { **hate** / **can't stand** } { peas. / eating peas. }

I'm sick (and tired) of your complaints.
I've had enough of your complaining.

▓ **Refusing**   (= saying that you won't do something)

I'm not going to / **I refuse to** } eat.

▓ **Giving Orders**   (= telling someone to do or not to do something)

You { **have to** / **have got to** } finish.

Stop / **Quit** } complaining.

C. Practice the following conversation with your partner.

A: What do you think about the new rent increase*?

B: <u>I'm against it</u>, of course! <u>It's not fair!</u>

A: <u>I agree with you! It's not necessary!</u>

B: In fact, <u>I'm in favor of</u> a rent decrease† instead!

A: A decrease? Are you kidding! No, <u>I don't agree with</u> you about a decrease. We'll never get a decrease. I just don't want to pay more rent than I do now.

Practice the conversation again. Use expressions from the following list instead of the underlined words.

▦ **Disagreeing**   (= expressing an opposite opinion)

I don't agree with ⎫
I disagree with   ⎬ you.

I'm against   ⎫
I'm opposed to ⎬ it.

It's not ⎰ fair.
         ⎱ right.

It's ⎰ not necessary.
     ⎱ unnecessary.

▦ **Agreeing**   (= expressing the same opinion)

I agree with you.
I think that you are right.

I'm ⎰ for   ⎱ it.
    ⎱ in favor of ⎰

---

*increase (n.) = higher amount
†decrease (n.) = smaller amount

D. Practice the following conversation with your partner.

A: Hey, <u>whose fault was</u> the accident? <u>It</u> definitely <u>wasn't my fault!</u>

B: Well, <u>don't blame me!</u> <u>It wasn't my fault!</u>

C: Okay, I admit that <u>I was responsible,</u> and <u>I'm really sorry. Please forgive me.</u> And don't worry, I have insurance. I promise that everything will be all right.

Practice the conversation again. Use expressions from the following list instead of the underlined words.

▨ **Blaming Someone for Something**   (= saying someone is responsible for something bad or wrong)

Whose fault is (was) it?	**It's (It was) (not) my fault.**
Who is (was) responsible for this?	**I'm (I was) (not) responsible.**
Don't blame me!	
Don't point the finger at me!	

▨ **Apologizing**   (= saying you are sorry about something)

I'm really sorry.	**Please forgive me.**
I apologize.	**Please accept my apologies.**

E. Now role play the situations in this section. Use your own words and the appropriate body language. How do you feel in each situation?

▨▨▨▨ EXPRESSING YOURSELF

A. **How Do They Feel?** Find a partner. Ask and answer questions about the story at the beginning of the chapter. Use *feel, look,* or *act.*

EXAMPLE: **Picture 1**
  1. **How does the manager look?   He looks nervous.**
  2. **Why?   . . . because the supervisor is visiting today.**

B. **What Do You Do?** Work with your partner. Take turns answering the following questions. Answer in complete sentences, using *when* and the vocabulary below. (Use each answer only once.)

get nervous	get angry (mad)	argue
get upset	discuss	complain
blame	apologize	lose one's temper

SITUATION: The bus is late.

EXAMPLE: [ask] **What do you do when the bus is late?**
          [answer] **When the bus is late, I get mad.**

---

1. Someone takes your parking space.

2. You have to go to a job interview.

3. You step on someone's foot by accident.

4. Your car doesn't start.

5. Your neighbor is playing loud music after midnight.

6. You disagree with someone's opinion about politics.

7. You get a parking ticket.

8. Someone borrows your car and has an accident.

9. There is a problem in your family.

⊞⊞⊞⊞ ROLE PLAY

Work with a partner.
Choose one of the following situations.
Each student plays one role.
Read and think only about your role.
How do you feel?
Act out the situations. Use expressions from this chapter.
(Your teacher may ask a third student to direct and give suggestions.)

Role A	Role B
1. You are a new waiter or waitress in a restaurant. First you serve a customer the wrong kind of soup. Then you bring cold soup. You apologize each time you make a mistake.	1. You are the customer. First you are annoyed and then you get mad about the second mistake. Finally, you complain about the service to the waiter or waitress.
2. You are a parent. You ask your teenager to clean up his or her room before dinner. When he or she refuses, you discuss the problem.	2. You are the teenager. You are watching TV and don't want to clean up your room. You think your parent is bothering you about something that is not really important.
3. You are a salesperson in a gift shop. You think a certain customer has just broken an expensive vase. You complain to the customer.	3. You are the customer. You blame another customer, a parent with a young child, for the broken vase. The parent and child are walking away from the broken vase.
4. You have just paid cash for an old used car. Now the car doesn't start. You complain to the sales-person.	4. You are the car salesperson. You are polite, but you don't want to give back the money. You argue that the customer bought the car "as is."
5. You are at a party, talking about politics. You are a non-smoker. There is a new tax on cigarettes, and you tell your friend that you are for it.	5. You are a smoker talking to your nonsmoker friend. You are against the new tax on cigarettes because you don't want to pay more for cigarettes.
6. (your own situation) ?	6. (your own situation) ?

⊠⊠⊠⊠ INTERVIEW

Ask your partner the following questions. Take notes on the answers. (Your teacher may ask you to do this exercise in groups of three or four.)

1. Do you ever get angry? What do you sometimes get angry about?

_____

EXAMPLE: [say] **I usually get angry about parking tickets.**

_____

2. Is there someone who often makes you mad? Who and why?
3. After you get angry, are you sorry?
4. In your opinion, is it healthier to express yourself or hold back your feelings when you are angry?
5. What kind of temper do you have? Do you have a bad (hot) temper? Do you get mad easily, or do you stay cool and calm?
6. When was the last time you lost your temper? What did you do?
7. After you lost your temper, did you regret it? Why or why not?
8. When you think you are going to lose your temper, what can you do instead?

Now change partners. Ask your new partner the same questions about his or her first partner. Use the third person, as in this example:

_____

EXAMPLE: When does he or she get angry?

[say] **She gets angry** { **when she gets a parking ticket.**
{ **when she loses her keys,** etc.

_____

⊠⊠⊠⊠ ONE STEP FURTHER

GAME: "GUESS WHO?"

You will need 3″ by 5″ cards for this game.

1. Do *not* write your name on the card.
2. Think about the last time you got angry. On one side of the card, answer this question: "Why did you get angry?"

_____

EXAMPLE: [write] I got angry because I lost my keys.

_____

3. On the other side of the card, if possible, answer this question: "Whose fault was it?"

_____

EXAMPLE: [write] It was my fault.

_____

4. Do *not* show your answers to anyone.

5. One student will collect the cards.

6. The teacher will read the cards aloud.

7. The students will try to guess who wrote each card.

8. After five wrong guesses, the student who wrote the card must identify himself or herself.

▦▦▦ PROBLEM SOLVING

Read the situation and possible solutions to yourself.
Which is the best solution? Write 1 next to the best idea, 2 next to the second best idea, and so forth.
Then work in groups of three or four.
Choose a secretary for your group.
Discuss your answers. Decide as a group the best order of the solutions.
The group secretary may write down the numbers.
Compare the answers of the different groups in the class.
Discuss why you chose certain solutions.

SITUATION: After interviewing several people, you choose a new roommate. He or she promises to be quiet and reliable, but during the first month your new roommate has two loud parties. Then he or she doesn't pay the rent on time. You are very upset.

WHAT SHOULD YOU DO?

a. _____ Tell your roommate that you are very disappointed. Warn that the next time he or she is noisy or late with the rent, you will ask him or her to move out.

b. _____ Lie and say that a friend wants to move in. Tell your new roommate to move out immediately.

c. _____ Complain loudly to your roommate's friend about the problem. Ask him or her to tell your roommate that you are angry.

d. _____ Be very polite. Don't show your roommate that you are upset. During the next party, get very mad, lose your temper, and angrily tell your roommate to move out.

e. _____ Forgive your roommate for these problems. Blame yourself for the situation and decide to live with your mistake, even if it makes you very unhappy.

f. _____ Be honest with your roommate. Try to work out an agreement about the noise and the rent. Give him or her a second chance.

g. _____ (your own solution)_____

_____

_____

⊠⊠⊠⊠ WORDPLAY

A. **Prepositions.** Complete the story with the correct prepositions. Use *at, about, for, to,* or *with*.

What a day! When I arrived this morning, the manager was really **nervous** ___about___ the supervisor's monthly visit. First he
                                    1
got very **annoyed** _____ a clerk because he was eating a
                              2
doughnut at his desk. Next he got **mad** _____ me and
                                                      3
another secretary because we were not working.

Then I heard some loud talking at the front of the bank. A
customer was **arguing** _____ a teller _____
                                    4   5
a mistake on her deposit slip. But the teller **apologized**

_____ her and said it wasn't her fault. She **blamed** the
          6
computer _____ the mistake. Soon the other customers in
                    7
line were **complaining** _____ the long wait also.
                                    8

Finally the boss got very **angry** _____ the computer
                                                9
repair company on the phone. He **lost his temper** because of the
broken computer. Then a funny thing happened. While he was **yelling**

_____ the person on the phone, the supervisor walked into
          10
the bank. Of course, the boss immediately started smiling at him and
acting very happy.

B. **Sentence Completion.** Make sentences from these words. Add
prepositions and other words you need. Use the past or past continuous
tense, as appropriate.

_____

EXAMPLE: manager / be / nervous / supervisor's / visit
[write] The manager was nervous about
            the supervisor's visit.

_____

1. manager / be / annoyed / clerk / because / he / eat

   _____

2. manager / be / mad / secretaries / because / they / not / work

   _____

3. customer / be / upset / mistake / on / deposit slip

   _____

4. customer / argue / teller / mistake

   _____

5. teller / blame / computer / mistake

   _____

6. other / customers / complain / long wait

   _____

7. boss / lose / his temper / because / he / be / angry / computer repair company

   _____

8. boss / yell / when / supervisor / arrive

   _____

C. **Parts of Speech**. Complete the story. Use the correct forms of the words.

discussion = noun   **discuss** = verb

1. One day at "The Sombrero" restaurant, two waiters were
    discussing Mexican cooking in the kitchen.

2. I was listening to part of their _____ .

---

argument = noun   **argue** = verb

---

3. They started to _____ about tortillas, the traditional flat Mexican corn bread.

4. One said, "You can't eat Mexican food without tortillas!" The other disagreed with him. Their _____ became very loud.

---

complaint = noun   **complain** = verb

---

5. Finally a customer _____ to the manager about the noise.

6. The manager told the waiters about the _____ .

---

apology = noun   **apologize** = verb   **apologetically** = adverb

---

7. One of the waiters _____ to the manager immediately.

8. Then he explained the argument to the customer _____ .

9. The customer kindly accepted his _____ .

---

anger = noun   **angry** = adjective   **angrily** = adverb

---

10. But the other waiter, who liked tortillas, got very _____ .

11. "I quit," he yelled _____ , and he walked out the door.

12. I still don't understand the reason for his _____ . Do you?

DISCUSSION (optional)

1. What is the traditional food of your culture?

2. What is your favorite dish?

3. Do you eat your culture's traditional food? How often?

4. Which kinds of American food do you, or don't you, like?

5. Is food in the United States and Canada as fresh and delicious as food in your country?

6. Do you like "junk food" (potato chips, french fries, candy, or soda, for example)?

CHAPTER 5
COURAGE

▦▦▦▦ TO THE RESCUE!

Look at the pictures and vocabulary words. Talk about what is happening in each picture.

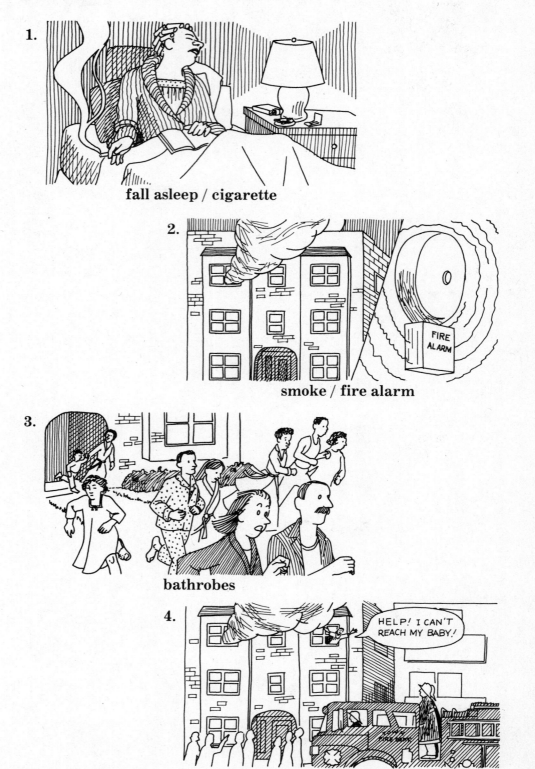

1. **fall asleep / cigarette**

2. **smoke / fire alarm**

3. **bathrobes**

4. HELP! I CAN'T REACH MY BABY!

fire truck

5.

jump / net

6.

fireman / ladder

7.

8. MOTHER GRATEFUL TO A BRAVE FIREFIGHTER

headline / mayor / medal

▨▨▨ WORDS AND EXPRESSIONS

expression	example
warn someone { **about** / **of** } something (= tell someone to be careful about a dangerous situation)	*She warned me { about the storm. / of the danger. }*
rescue someone **from** something or somewhere (= help someone get away from danger)	*They rescued the cat from the roof.*
save { someone **from** something / someone's **life** } (= rescue someone from death)	*The park ranger saved me from the bear.* *After the accident, a nurse saved my life.*
risk one's **life for** someone (= put one's own life in danger to save another person's life)	*He risked his life for the child.*
be { **brave** / **courageous** } (= not to be afraid)	*Some soldiers are very { brave. / courageous. }*
be a hero or **heroine** (= act very bravely)	*He was a hero in the war.* *She was a heroine in the story.*
escape from someone or something (= get away from danger)	*We escaped from the fire.*
call for help	*The drowning child called for help.*
admire / **respect** } { someone **for** + VERB*ing* / something } **look up to** someone (= have a high opinion of someone)	*I admire* / *I respect* } { *you for stating your opinion.* / *your point of view.* } *I look up to my parents.*
praise someone **for** { + VERB*ing* / something } (= say good things about someone)	*She praised him for { saving her life. / his courage. }*
be { **grateful** / **thankful** } **to** someone **for** { + VERB*ing* / something } (= feel or show thanks to someone)	*I'm grateful to you for { helping me. / your help. }*
dare to + VERB (= be brave enough to do something)	*She dared to ask her boss for a raise.*
dare someone **to** + VERB (= challenge someone to do something)	*He dared her to drive faster.*

expression	example
cause an accident (= make an accident happen)	*A drunk driver caused the accident.*
by accident **accidentally** (= opposite of **on purpose**, not planned)	*The fire started* { *by accident.* *accidentally.*
be } **have** } **a close call** (= have a narrow escape from danger or failure)	*That was a close call!* } *We had a close call!* } *We almost hit that dog.*
be a lifesaver (= save someone from difficulty)	*You're a lifesaver! I'm thirsty and you brought water.*
arrive in the nick of time (= reach someone or someplace just before it is too late)	*The ambulance arrived just in the nick of time to rescue the dying man.*

▨▨▨▨ TELLING THE STORY

Look at the picture story to answer these questions. Pay special attention to the words **in dark type**.

1. What **causes** the fire?
2. Who or what **warns** the people **about** the fire?
3. Why is the woman **calling for help**?
4. How does the woman finally **escape from** the flames?
5. Who **saves** the baby's **life**?
6. How does he **rescue** the baby from the smoke?
7. Why does the firefighter **risk his life** to save the baby?
8. Is the firefighter **a hero**? Why is the mother **grateful to** him?

▨▨▨▨ FINISHING THE STORY

1. When the child is older, do you think her mother will tell her about the fire?
2. Will she meet the person who saved her life?
3. Will they become friends?

▣▣▣▣ BODY LANGUAGE

A. Courage is a way of acting in a dangerous situation. The following
   words are used in rescue operations. Match each picture with a
   description of the action. Write the correct letter on the line.

A.

1. _____ **climb up** or **down**

2. _____ **throw** } something **to** someone
       toss

B.

3. _____ **reach for** something

4. _____ **grab** } **(hold of)** something
       take

5. _____ **hold (onto)** something
       not let go of someone

C.
FIRE
ESCAPE

B. Work in pairs. Cover the words. Look only at the pictures. Describe
   where each person is and what he or she is doing.

D.
ROPE

_____

EXAMPLE: Picture C
   1. Where is he?   He's on the fire escape.
   2. What's he doing?   He's climbing up the fire escape.

E.
LIFE
PRESERVER

_____

C. In groups, make a list of **natural disasters.**
   (Your teacher may ask each group to write its list on the blackboard.)

_____

EXAMPLES: earthquakes, floods, forest fires, etc.

_____

Discuss various ways people rescue the victims of these disasters.

▨▨▨▨ EXPRESSIONS AND CONVERSATIONS

A. Practice the following conversation with your partner. Use the appropriate body language to act out (dramatize) the situation.

A: Hey! <u>Watch out!</u> A rock is falling! Quick! <u>Move!</u>
The rock hits the climber.

B: Oh, no! <u>Help!</u> Oh, my arm!

A: <u>Are you hurt?</u> Okay, <u>don't move!</u> You might have a broken shoulder. I'll be right there.

B: Hurry up, please! <u>It hurts!</u> Come quickly.

A: Shhh...<u>be quiet.</u> I'm coming right now.

B. Now practice the conversation again. Use different expressions for the underlined words. Have several different conversations.

EXAMPLE: [instead of] Watch out!
                    [say] **Look out!**

▨ **Giving a Warning**   (= telling someone to be careful of danger)

Watch out!   **Get out of the way!**
Look out!   **Move!**

Keep ⎫ **still!**   **Be** ⎫ **quiet!**
Be ⎭   **Keep** ⎭
Don't move!   **Don't talk!**

▨ **Calling for Help**

Help!   **Are you hurt?**   **I'm in pain.**
Help me!   **Are you injured?**   **It hurts.**

C. Practice the following conversation with your partner.

PARENT: My child! Oh, thank god he's alive! <u>Thank you so much!</u>

LIFEGUARD*: Believe me, <u>it was nothing, really.</u> I was just doing my job.

PARENT: Well, <u>I really appreciate your help!</u> <u>I can't thank you enough!</u>

LIFEGUARD: <u>Don't mention it. Glad to be of assistance.</u>

Practice the conversation again. Use expressions from the following list instead of the underlined words.

▣ **Thanking Someone**

Thank you { **very much!** / **so much!** }   **I really appreciate** / **I'm very grateful for** } your help.

How can I thank you?
I can't thank you enough.

▣ **Accepting Thanks**

You're welcome.
Don't mention it.   **It was nothing, really.**
It was my pleasure.

Glad to be of { **assistance.** / **help.** }

---

*lifeguard (n.) = person who rescues drowning people

D. Practice the following conversation with your partner.

A: <u>I bet you can't ask</u> _____* to dance. You're too shy and _____ is too popular.

B: Oh, yeah? Well, <u>I'll show you.</u> I'm not too shy! How much do you want to bet? I'm going to ask _____ to dance right now!

A: Okay, <u>prove it.</u> I bet you five dollars. <u>I dare you to</u> do it!

B: Okay, <u>no problem!</u> It's a deal. <u>Just you wait and see!</u> Here I go!

Practice the conversation again. Use expressions from the following list instead of the underlined words.

▨ **Challenging Someone**   (= trying to make someone do something dangerous or difficult)

I bet you can't jump over that.   **Prove it!**
I dare you to drive faster.   **Show me!**

▨ **Accepting a Challenge**

I'll prove it to you.   **No problem!**
I'll show you.   **Easy!**

Just you wait and see!
Just watch me!

E. Now role play the situations in this section. Use your own words and appropriate body language. How do you feel in each situation?

_____
*_____ = the name of a classmate

▓▓▓▓ EXPRESSING YOURSELF

What Should You Do? Work with a partner. Take turns asking and answering the following questions. Answer in complete sentences, using *if* and an appropriate solution from the following list or one of your own.

SOLUTIONS

a. Take a deep breath and try not to look at the audience.
b. Try to build a fire and wait for help.
c. Go to the basement.
d. Stay calm and press the emergency alarm button.
e. Take your time and practice what you are going to say.
f. Try to stay in the shade and wait for help.
g. Call the fire department immediately.
h. Get under a table or stand in a doorway.
i. See a doctor as soon as you can.

SITUATION: You see a fire.

EXAMPLE: [ask] **What should you do if you see a fire?**
             [answer] **If you see a fire, you should call the fire department immediately.**

---

1. Your car runs out of* gas in the desert.

2. You get very nervous before you're going to give a speech.

3. A snake bites your hand.

4. A tornado is coming toward your house.

5. You feel an earthquake.

6. You are lost in a snowstorm in the mountains.

7. You are stuck in a broken elevator; you can't get out.

8. You feel uncomfortable before an important phone call.

---

*run out of (v.) = not have any more

▨▨▨▨ ROLE PLAY

Work with a partner.
Choose one of the following situations.
Each student plays one role.
Read and think only about your role.
How do you feel?
Act out the situations. Use expressions from this chapter.
(Your teacher may ask a third student to direct and give suggestions.)

Role A	Role B
1. You are a grateful parent. A safety patrol person rescued your child from a close call at the corner this morning. A car almost hit your child. You call to thank him or her.	1. You are the safety patrol person. You accept the thanks but explain that you were only doing your job. You are also very glad that the child was not hurt.
2. You are a new student in class. You are afraid to write your auto-biography (story of your life) in English because you are very shy. You hate writing about yourself.	2. You sit next to the new student. You bet him or her that he or she can write a good paper. You explain that an autobiography doesn't have to be extremely personal. You can just write the facts.
3. You are riding a bicycle with a friend. Suddenly you see a hole in the sidewalk and you warn your friend to be careful.	3. You don't turn in time to avoid the hole. You fall off the bicycle and hurt your leg. You complain about the pain and ask your friend to help you get up.
4. You have your first job inter-view in English, and you are very nervous and scared. After your friend tells you to be confident, you feel better.	4. You have some experience with job interviews in English. You tell your friend to relax, and bet him or her that he will get the job.
5. (your own situation) ?	5. (your own situation) ?

▦▦▦▦ INTERVIEW

Ask your partner the following questions. Take notes on the answers.
(Your teacher may ask you to do this exercise in groups of three or four.)

1. Have you (or has anyone you know) ever been in a dangerous
    situation? Describe what happened. Did anyone rescue you?

    _____

    EXAMPLE: [say] **Yes, once I was in an automobile accident, and the police
    rescued me.**
    _____

2. Have you (or has anyone you know) ever rescued anyone from a
    dangerous situation? What happened? Tell the story.

3. Are there stories in your culture or religion about famous heroes
    and heroines? Give some examples. Why are they famous? What
    did they do?

4. When you have to do something difficult or dangerous (for
    example, give a speech in English, swim across a river), how do
    you prepare yourself mentally or emotionally?

5. Does it take courage to leave behind your own culture and move to
    a new country? Why?

6. If you don't know the language in a new country, it can be
    dangerous. Describe one situation where it could be dangerous.

7. When your opinion is different from most of your classmates', do
    you dare tell them? Or do you remain silent? Why?

8. In your culture, is it acceptable to have your own opinion about
    something, or is it usually better to agree with the popular
    opinion?

Now change partners. Ask your new partner the same questions about
his or her first partner. Use the third person, as in this example:

_____

EXAMPLE: Has he ever been in a dangerous situation? Did anyone rescue him?
    [say] **Yes, he's been in a dangerous situation before, and the
    police rescued him.**
_____

▦▦▦▦ ONE STEP FURTHER

GAME: "BE BRAVE"

You will need 3″ by 5″ cards for this game.

1. Your teacher will write each vocabulary word from the list of
    natural disasters you made in Exercise C on page 70 on separate 3″
    by 5″ cards. (Additional words from the **Body Language** section
    may be added.)

2. Each student must pick one card.

3. After you pick your card, *do not show it* to anyone! Think about how you can demonstrate the meaning of the word through your actions, without speaking. (If there are many students, two partners can work together.)

4. The teacher will call on students in alphabetical order. When it is your turn, act out the word in front of the class. Students will try to guess what your word is.

5. After the class guesses the word, continue to the next person.

▦▦▦▦ PROBLEM SOLVING

Read the situation and possible solutions to yourself.
Which is the best solution? Write 1 next to the best idea, 2 next to the second best idea, and so forth.
Then work in groups of three or four.
Choose a secretary for your group.
Discuss your answers. Decide as a group the best order of the solutions.
The group secretary may write down the numbers.
Compare the answers of the different groups in the class.
Discuss why you chose certain solutions.

SITUATION: You and a friend are swimming at the beach. You are close to the shore, and your friend is in deep water. Other swimmers are nearby. Suddenly your friend screams. He or she sees a large gray fish with big teeth swimming in your direction.

WHAT SHOULD YOU DO?

a. _____ Panic when your friend screams. Start yelling "Help!" and waving your arms. Swim away from the shore.

b. _____ Warn the other swimmers immediately. Start calling for help. Swim quickly in the direction of the shore.

c. _____ Risk your life to save your friend. Let the shark follow you away from the shore. After your friend is safe, escape to safety yourself.

d. _____ Decide maybe the fish is not a shark and not dangerous. Touch the fish and dare your friend to do the same. When your friend accepts the challenge, praise him or her for his or her courage.

e. _____ Get out of the water immediately. Find a lifeguard to rescue your friend and the other swimmers who are in danger.

f. _____ (your own solution)_____

_____

_____

▦▦▦▦ WORDPLAY

A. **Prepositions.** Complete the story with the correct preposition. Use *about, of, for, from,* or *to.*

Early yesterday morning, a fire alarm at 1321 Sea View St. **warned** the residents ___about___ a fire on the third floor. When

[1]

the fire engine arrived, a woman on the second floor was **calling** _____ **help.** She was trying to **save** her baby

[2]

_____ the smoke in the next room. Finally, she jumped

[3]

into a net to **escape** _____ the flames.

[4]

Immediately afterward, a fireman on a ladder climbed into the room and bravely **rescued** the baby _____ the fire. The

[5]

brave firefighter **risked** his **life** _____ the baby. Of

[6]

course, the overjoyed mother was very **grateful** _____

[7]

him _____ his courageous actions. Later, fire inspectors

[8]

said that a cigarette had started the fire.

B. **Sentence Completion.** Make sentences from these words. Add prepositions and other words you need. Use the past or past continuous tense, as appropriate.

_____

EXAMPLE: What / cause / fire / ?
 [write] What caused the fire?

_____

1. alarm / warn / people / fire

_____

2. woman / on / third floor / call / help

_____

3. woman / jump / to escape / flames

_____

4. fireman / rescue / baby / smoke

_____

5. why / do / fireman / risk / his life / save / baby / ?

_____

6. mayor / give / fireman / medal / for / his courage

_____

7. mother / be / grateful / fireman / because / he / save / baby

_____

C. **Parts of Speech.** Complete the story. Use the correct forms of the words.

Welcome to eight hours of Traffic Safety class today! If you give me your complete attention, I think we will have a very interesting day!

_____

safety = noun   **safe** = adjective   **safely** = adverb

_____

1. We all know how important it is to have ____**safe**____ highways, don't we?

2. Well, today we are going to talk about traffic _____ .

3. We're going to discuss how to drive _____ .

---

danger = noun   **dangerous** = adjective   **dangerously** = adverb

---

4. Don't forget! Every time you get into a car, your life is in
   _____ .

5. There are millions of _____ drivers on our streets
   and freeways.

6. If you see someone who is driving _____ , what
   should you do? Be careful! The driver may be drunk.

Point 1: Never drink and drive! And watch out for drunk drivers!

---

risk = noun   **risk** = verb   **risky** = adjective

---

7. After an accident, it's always very _____ to try to
   rescue someone from a burning car.

8. Don't forget! If you go near a burning car, you are taking a big
   _____ . Please, wait for the fire department and don't
   _____ your life.

Point 2: Never go near a burning car!

---

warning = noun   **warn** = verb

---

9. I should also _____ you about one more thing
   concerning accidents.

10. Please pay attention to this final _____ !

---

bravery = noun   **brave** = adjective   **bravely** = adverb

---

11. Of course, it is admirable to act _____ and try to save
    the life of an injured person in an accident.

12. Be _____ , but don't be impatient. Wait for the
    paramedics! They know how to move an injured person the right
    way.

13. Sometimes, it's more important to act with caution* than with
    _____ .

Point 3: Never move an injured person!

---

*caution (n.) = carefulness

CHAPTER 6

FEAR

⊞⊞⊞⊞ SCARY BUSINESS

Look at the pictures and vocabulary words. Talk about what is happening in each picture.

1.

hill / sign

2.

real estate agent* / lightning

3.

spider web / ghost

4.

portrait / mice

5.

dark

6.

candle / skeleton

7.

bats

8.

stairway

---

*real estate agent (n.) = property salesperson

❖❖❖❖ WORDS AND EXPRESSIONS

expression	example
be nervous about { + VERB*ing* / something } (= feel uncertain, a little afraid or excited)	*I'm nervous about* { *taking my driving test.* / *the plane trip.* }
be worried about { + VERB*ing* / someone or something } (= be afraid something bad will happen or has happened)	*He's worried about losing his camera.* *He's worried about Ken; he's not home yet.*
be a worrywart (= worry all the time)	*Don't pay any attention to her; she's a worrywart.*
be { **scared** / **scared to death** / **afraid** } **of** { + VERB*ing* / someone or something } **to** + VERB something (= feel fear)	*They're afraid of thieves.* *I'm* { *scared* / *scared to death* } { *of walking home alone at night.* / *to walk home alone at night.* }
frighten } someone **scare** (= make someone afraid)	*Your Dracula mask* { *frightened* / *scared* } *everyone at the party.*
scare someone **out of their wits** (= frighten someone severely)	*The loud noise scared me out of my wits!*
be { **scary** / **frightening** } (= cause fear)	*You should see Blood! It is a* { *scary* / *frightening* } *movie.*
be { **frightened** / **terrified** / **petrified** } **of** { + VERB*ing* / someone or something } (= be extremely afraid)	*They're* { *frightened of flying in an airplane.* / *terrified of ghosts.* }
hesitate to + VERB (= pause before an action)	*She hesitated to enter the dark room.*
dread { + VERB*ing* / something } (= be extremely afraid)	*I dread* { *going to the dentist.* / *my final exam.* }
shock someone (= cause a strong negative reaction)	*His crazy behavior at the party shocked me.*
be { **horrible** / **awful** / **tragic** / **terrible** / **dreadful** } (= cause fear and shock)	*The story about her experiences in the war was horrible.*
panic (= feel sudden fear and loss of control)	*I panicked when I could not open the elevator door.*

expression	example
be { **strange** / **weird** } (= be unusual or disturbing)	*The man holding that snake looks really strange.* *The noises coming from that room are weird.*
be creepy (slang) (= be strange)	*The movie about the "killer mouse" was creepy.*
give someone **the creeps** (slang) (= make someone feel strange)	*Yeah, it gave me the creeps.*
sneak { **up on** someone / **away from** someone } (= move quietly so no one hears or sees)	*Let's sneak up on Terry and scare him.* *The robber is sneaking away from the police.*
hide { something / **from** someone } (= put something where on one can see or find it)	*He hid the money under the bed.* *Now the robber is hiding from the police.*

▨▨▨▨ TELLING THE STORY

Look at the picture story to answer these questions. Pay special attention to the words **in dark type.**

1. How does the house look at first? Why does it look **strange** during the storm?
2. What are the couple **frightened of** in the hall?
3. Why does the wife **sneak away from** the living room?
4. Where is the ghost **hiding** in the living room?
5. Is the husband **afraid of** ghosts?
6. Why do the lights go out? Does the real estate agent, Mr. Drake, act **frightened**? Why or why not?
7. Why are the couple **terrified of** the painting?
8. What flying things **scare** them next?

▨▨▨▨ FINISHING THE STORY

1. Will the couple ever go near the house again?
2. Will they call Castle Real Estate to complain about their frightening experience?
3. Will they have nightmares (bad dreams) about the house?

✜✜✜✜ BODY LANGUAGE

A. Match each picture with a description of the action. Write the correct letter on the line.

A.

1. _____ sweat

2. _____ tremble with fear
   shake (in one's boots)
   shiver

B.

3. _____ turn { white as a sheet
              { pale as a ghost

4. _____ gulp / gasp (for air)
   (= breathe in air and make a sudden noise)

C.

5. _____ pass out or faint

6. _____ crawl (away)

D.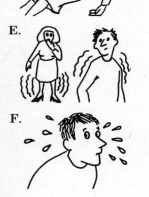

B. Work in pairs. Cover the words. Look only at the pictures. Describe what each person is doing and why. (Make up your explanations.)

E.

EXAMPLE: Picture C
   1. What's he doing?   He's crawling away.
   2. Why?   ...because he's afraid.
   **   ...because he saw a ghost.**

F.

C. In groups, talk about cultural differences. Answer these questions:

1. Do people in your culture show their feelings of fear in the same ways as in the pictures?

2. In what other ways do they express fear?

3. In your culture, do people expect girls to be more afraid than boys? What about men and women?

Summarize your discussion for the class.

▦▦▦▦ EXPRESSIONS AND CONVERSATIONS

A. Practice the following conversation with your partner. Use the appropriate body language to act out (dramatize) the situation.

CHILD: Help me, Mommy (Daddy), don't let go! <u>I'm afraid of</u> the water.

PARENT: <u>Don't worry!</u> Just hold onto my hands.

CHILD: But I <u>can't</u> swim.

PARENT: Okay, <u>just relax</u>. I'll help you. You know <u>you can trust me</u>.

B. Now practice the conversation again. Use different expressions for the underlined words. Have several conversations.

EXAMPLE: [instead of] I'm afraid of the water.
          [say] **I'm scared of the water.**

▦ **Expressing Fear: Inability**   (= fear because you are unable to do something)

I'm $\left\{ \begin{array}{l} \textbf{afraid of} \\ \textbf{scared of} \end{array} \right\}$ the water.

I $\left\{ \begin{array}{l} \textbf{can't} \\ \textbf{don't know how to} \end{array} \right\}$ swim.

▦ **Comforting Someone**   (= helping someone not to feel afraid)

Don't worry.   You can trust me.
There's nothing to worry about.   You can count on me.

Just relax.
Don't get upset.

C. Practice the following conversation with your partner.

A: We <u>should</u> leave now. It's getting dark.

B: <u>Shhh! Be quiet!</u> I just heard something over there! *(whisper)* <u>Don't move!</u>

A: Come on, let's <u>get out of here!</u>

B: <u>Shhh! Stop talking!</u>...Oh, never mind*! It's just a snake.

Practice the conversation again. Use expressions from the following list instead of the underlined words.

▣ Giving Orders

Don't move!	Quit ⎱ **talking!**
Stop!	**Stop** ⎰
Stay ⎱ **still!**	**Shhh! Be quiet!**
Keep ⎰	

▣ Making Suggestions

We **should** leave.
I **ought to** go.
You **had better** get going.

Let's ⎰ **leave!**
     ⎱ **get out of here!**

D. Practice the following conversation with your partner.

A: Hey, wake up! Look over there. <u>You won't believe it!</u>

B: <u>Oh, no! It's horrible!</u> What is it?

A: It's some kind of huge animal. Oh, no! It's looking at us! <u>Don't panic!</u>

B: <u>I'm not panicking.</u> Where's the camera? Quick!

A: Whew, it's running away! Now we can relax. <u>It's all right now.</u>

Practice the conversation again. Use expressions from the following list instead of the underlined words.

▣ Expressing Shock

Oh, no!
Oh, my gosh!

It's ⎰ **horrible!**
    ⎱ **awful!**

You won't believe it!
It's unbelievable!

▣ Reassuring Someone (= helping someone to recover from a shock)

Don't panic!	**It's all right now.**
Stay calm!	**Everything is okay.**
I'm not panicking.	
I'm staying calm.	

*Never mind = Forget it. It's not important.

E. Now role play the situations in this section. Use your own words and the appropriate body language. How do you feel in each situation?

▨▨▨▨ EXPRESSING YOURSELF

A. **What Do You Say?** Use these expressions in your answers to the questions that follow.

EXPRESSIONS

Why are you so nervous?

Don't be such a worrywart.

That gave me the creeps.

What a tragic story!

I'm dreading every minute of it.

Don't panic!

How strange...

It shocked all of us!

Don't hesitate to call me.

EXAMPLE: What do you say when a person thinks only about what can go wrong?

[say] **Don't be such a worrywart.**

WHAT DO YOU SAY?

1. ...when you find out your depressed friend is going to be alone all weekend?

2. ...after you see a scary movie that gives you nightmares?

3. ...when an elevator breaks and you are caught inside with several other people?

4. ...when there is a murder* in your neighborhood?

5. ...when your friend can't sit still and relax?

6. ...when you have to take a two-hour exam tomorrow?

7. ...when the phone rings and you pick it up but no one answers?

8. ...when you hear a true story about someone losing his or her family in a war?

---

*murder (n.) = a killing

B. **What Are You Afraid Of?** Work with a partner. Take turns asking and answering questions. Answer in complete sentences. Use *afraid of*, *frightened of*, or *scared of* in your questions and answers.

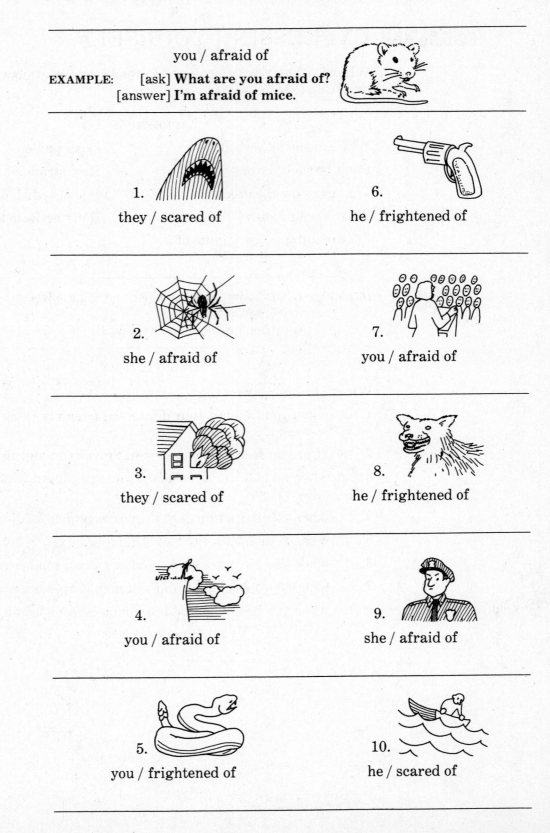

you / afraid of

EXAMPLE: [ask] **What are you afraid of?**
[answer] **I'm afraid of mice.**

1. they / scared of

6. he / frightened of

2. she / afraid of

7. you / afraid of

3. they / scared of

8. he / frightened of

4. you / afraid of

9. she / afraid of

5. you / frightened of

10. he / scared of

▓▓▓▓ ROLE PLAY

Work in pairs.
Choose one of the following situations.
Each student plays one role.
Read and think only about your role.
How do you feel?
Act out the situations. Use expressions from this chapter.
(Your teacher may ask a third student to direct and give suggestions.)

Role A	**Role B**
1. You are a new student, and you have to give your first speech in front of the class. You are nervous and panicking.	1. You are the teacher. You encourage your student to relax and give the speech, because you believe he or she can do a good job.
2. Your child wakes up with a high fever. She is crying and her face is hot and red. You call the doctor's office and talk to the nurse.	2. You are the nurse. You tell the parent of the sick child not to worry. You ask him or her to put a cold towel on the child's head and bring her to the doctor right away.
3. You are an experienced instructor in a driving school. You are teaching a new student how to drive a car. You reassure your student that he or she can learn easily.	3. You are the student. This is your first driving lesson. You don't know how to drive and are very afraid because you have been in an accident before. But you have to learn how to drive for your job.
4. You live in a dangerous area. You are alone late one night when you hear someone on the roof. You get very scared and call the police.	4. You are the police officer. You tell the person on the phone not to worry. You explain that someone will be there very soon to help.
5. (your own situation) ?	5. (your own situation) ?

▧▧▧▧ INTERVIEW

Ask your partner the following questions. Take notes on the answers. (Your teacher may ask you to do this exercise in groups of three or four.)

1. When you were a child, what (or who) were you afraid of?

_____

EXAMPLE: [say] **When I was a child, I was afraid of the dark.**

_____

2. What (or who) still frightens you now?

3. Do you get nervous before taking exams? What usually makes you nervous?

4. Do you think that "city people" are afraid of the same things as "country people"? Discuss the differences.

5. Are you afraid of driving on the freeway? When you get into a car, do you use your seat belt?

6. Are you afraid of crime where you live now? Is it dangerous to go out alone at night in your neighborhood? If you are from another country, do you feel the same way there?

7. Do you ever go to horror movies? Why or why not? In your opinion, should young children see scary movies? Why or why not?

8. In the United States, some people believe the spirits of dead people, or ghosts, visit earth on Halloween night (October 31). Children dress in scary costumes to celebrate Halloween. Is there a similar holiday in your country? Describe it.

9. Do you ever worry about the future? What do you worry about the most?

Now change partners. Ask your new partner the same questions about his or her first partner. Use the third person, as in this example:

_____

EXAMPLE: What was she afraid of when she was a child?
[say] **When she was a child, she was afraid of the dark.**

_____

▧▧▧▧ ONE STEP FURTHER

GAME: "STORYTELLING"

You will need 3″ by 5″ cards for this game.

1. Sit in groups of four or five students. You are going to write a scary story together. Choose one student to be the secretary for your group.

2. First, each student in the group must individually answer each of the following questions in a complete sentence on the card.

   a. What time is it?
   b. Where are you?
   c. What are you doing?
   d. Suddenly something scary happens. What happens?
   e. How do you react? What do you do?

3. After you all finish, each student must read his or her answers to the group. Which answers are the best? Choose one student's story.

4. Work together. Tell the best story again but this time add more description. The secretary should write down the story. Don't forget—it must be a scary story! If there is time, the secretary from each group can read the story to the rest of the class.

▦▦▦▦ PROBLEM SOLVING

Read the situation and possible solutions to yourself.
Which is the best solution? Write 1 next to the best idea, 2 next to the second best idea, and so forth.
Then work in groups of three or four. Choose a secretary.
Discuss your answers. Decide as a group the best order of the solutions.
The group secretary may write down the numbers.
Compare the answers of the different groups in the class.
Discuss why you chose certain solutions.

SITUATION: You are a salesperson. You must travel on an airplane to another city every month. On your last trip, the plane had engine trouble and almost crashed. Now you are afraid to fly but you have to travel again next month.

WHAT SHOULD YOU DO?

a. _____ Try to stop worrying. Get on the plane, even if you feel so nervous that you won't be able to work when you arrive.

b. _____ Panic and cancel your flight. Tell your boss that you are ill. Think about changing jobs.

c. _____ Try to hide your fears by drinking alcohol. Arrive drunk for your business appointment.

d. _____ Don't tell your boss about your problem. Work with a counselor to overcome* your fear of flying.

e. _____ Explain your problem to your boss and ask for a short medical leave.

f. _____ (your own solution)_____

_____

_____

*overcome = solve a difficult problem

❖❖❖❖ WORDPLAY

A. **Prepositions.** Complete the story with the correct prepositions. Use *away, from, of, up, about,* or *to.*

Dear Animal Doc,

DEAR ANIMAL DOC

Jessica

I'm **worried** __about__ my cat, Samantha. I need some advice quickly! I hope you can help me. Here is the problem.

My cat is **afraid** _____ mice! Sometimes, she **sneaks** _____ on a mouse, but then she just **sneaks** _____ from it. She is also **scared** _____ **death** _____ dogs! When she sees a dog, she **hides** _____ it.

As a matter of fact, she is very **nervous** _____ other cats, too. When she sees another cat, she **hesitates** _____ play with it. She is also **frightened** _____ people, except me! I don't think this behavior* is normal for cats. Am I right?

Sincerely,

Jessica

B. **Sentence Completion.** Make sentences from these words. Add prepositions and other words you need. Use the past or past continuous tense, as appropriate.

EXAMPLE: house / look / scary / during / storm
[write] The house looked scary during the storm.

1. house / do not look / scary / before / storm

2. husband / wife / be / afraid / spiders / hall

*behavior (n.) = way of acting

3. ghost / hiding / visitors / behind / draperies / living room

_____

4. wife / try to / sneak / when / she / see / ghost

_____

5. when / lights / go out, / both / them / be / scared

_____

6. when / they / see / portrait, / husband / turn / pale / and / wife / faint

_____

7. both / them / scream / when / bats / fly / living room

_____

C. **Parts of Speech**. Complete the story. Use the correct forms of the words.

Sam is a rancher in Arizona. Last week he had to drive across the desert on a lonely dirt road to get to town. His son, Hank, sat next to him in his old truck. It was August and the weather was unusually hot.

_____

worried = adjective   **worry** = verb   **worriedly** = adverb

1. Young Hank looked __worried__ .
2. "How much gas do we have?" he asked again _____ .
3. "Don't _____ !" said Sam. "It'll be all right!" But the gas tank was empty.

_____

fear = noun   **afraid** = adjective   **fearfully** = adverb

4. Suddenly the old truck stopped. "Don't be _____ !" said Sam. Then he pointed to a sign: GAS – 1 MILE.
5. "But what if the station is closed?" Hank asked _____ .
6. "Son, _____ won't help us now," Sam laughed. "We need some luck instead!"

---

danger = noun   **dangerous** = adjective   **dangerously** = adverb

---

7. The situation was _____ . They had no gas and very little water.

8. When they reached the gas station, it was closed. The weather was _____ hot and dry.

9. Then Sam saw an old gas can inside the closed station. "We're out of _____ now!" he thought.

---

scare = noun   **scared** = adjective   **scare** = verb

---

10. He was right. The can was full of gas, and the _____ was over!

11. Later Hank asked Sam, "When you saw that closed station, weren't you just a little _____ ?"

12. Like a real cowboy, Sam answered, "Son, it takes more than that to _____ me."

DISCUSSION (optional)

1. How would you feel in a similar situation?
2. Have you ever seen an American cowboy? Where?
3. Do you like cowboy movies? Who is your favorite cowboy actor?

CHAPTER 7

LOVE

▦▦▦▦ RITA GROWS UP

Look at the pictures and vocabulary words. Talk about what is happening in each picture.

1.

tomboy* / baseball bat

2.

polish / convertible

3.

change oil / greasy

4.

change tire

---

*tomboy = girl who acts like a boy

5.

magazine

6.

grow up

7.

ring / propose

8.

honeymoon

▨▨▨▨ WORDS AND EXPRESSIONS

expression	example
like { someone or something / **to** + VERB / + VERB*ing* } (= feel interest or affection for a person or thing)	*I like that band.* *I like* { *to watch* / *watching* } *T.V.*
be fond of { someone or something / + VERB*ing* } (= like or love a person or thing)	*I'm very fond of* { *my teacher.* / *skiing.* }
(not) care for { someone or something / + VERB*ing* } (= (not) like or love a person or thing)	*I care for my parents.* *I don't care for swimming.*
get along / **be friendly** } **with** someone (= have a good relationship)	*I get along well with my boss.* *I am friendly with her.*
be { **nice** / **kind** } **to** someone (= help someone, be interested in the happiness of another person)	*He's very* { *nice* / *kind* } *to his parents.*
be { **thoughtful** / **considerate** } **to** + VERB (= think of other people's feelings)	*You were very* { *thoughtful* / *considerate* } *to visit me when I was sick.*
appreciate someone or something (= recognize the value of a person or thing)	*I really appreciate your help.*
be { **grateful** / **thankful** } **to** someone **for** { + VERB*ing* / something } (= feel appreciation for someone or something)	*I'm* { *grateful* / *thankful* } *to my teacher for* { *helping me.* / *her help.* }
admire / **respect** } { someone / something } **for** { + VERB*ing* / something } **look up to** someone (= have a high opinion of someone)	*I admire* { *you for being so honest.* / *your honesty.* } *I look up to my parents.*
be attracted to someone (= feel a strong interest)	*He's attracted to women with strong personalities.*
have a crush on someone (= be very attracted)	*He has a crush on one of his classmates.*
flirt with someone (= act in a way to attract the attention of the opposite sex)	*She flirted with your cute friend at the party.*

expression	example
date someone	*He's dating a friend of his sister.*
ask someone **out (for a date)**	*He asked your friend out (for a date).*
go out (on a date) with someone (= go out with someone of the opposite sex)	*She went out (on a date) with your friend last weekend.*
go steady with someone (= go out with or date only one person)	*We have been going steady for two months.*
love { someone or something + VERB*ing* **to** + VERB } (= have strong feelings of affection for a person; like a thing very much)	*I love my family.* *I love* { *listening to the radio.* *to listen.* }
be affectionate with someone (= show love by treating gently)	*He is very affectionate with his children.*
fall in love } **be in love** } **with** someone (= feel a strong attraction) (= have strong feelings of love)	*We fell in love last spring.* *We are still in love.*
fall head over heels in love with someone (= fall completely in love)	*The first time I saw you, I fell head over heels in love with you.*
propose to someone (= ask someone to marry)	*He proposed to her last year.*
get } **be** } **married to** someone	*They are getting married next month.* *They are still married after many years.*

▨▨▨▨ TELLING THE STORY

A. Look at the picture story. Underline the correct word(s) to complete each sentence.

EXAMPLE: Rita (cares for / <u>doesn't care for</u>) fancy dresses.

---

1. Rita (is / isn't) fond of baseball and cars.
2. Rita (admires / doesn't admire) Bill and his convertible.
3. Bill (is / isn't) attracted to Rita because she's a tomboy.
4. Bill (is / isn't) considerate to give Rita his old car magazines.
5. Bill (appreciates / doesn't appreciate) Rita's help.
6. When Rita grows up, she (flirts / doesn't flirt) with Bill.
7. Bill (falls / doesn't fall) in love with Rita when she comes back.
8. Bill and Rita (get married / don't get married) and drive away in Bill's convertible for their honeymoon.

B. How well did you understand the story? Don't look at the pictures. Write **T** if the statement is **true**, **F** if it is **false**.

EXAMPLE: __F__ Rita likes to wear girls' clothes.

---

1. _____ Rita doesn't care for baseball or convertibles.
2. _____ She looks up to Bill because he is taller than she is.
3. _____ Bill and Rita don't get along with each other.
4. _____ Rita has a crush on Bill.
5. _____ Bill isn't very attracted to Rita when she returns two years later.
6. _____ Bill falls head over heels in love with Rita.
7. _____ Rita proposes to Bill and he accepts.

C. Work with a partner. Explain or correct the false statements.

EXAMPLE: [say] **The example is false. Rita likes to wear boy's clothes.**

▨▨▨▨ BODY LANGUAGE

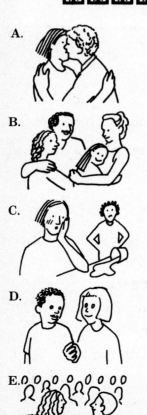

A.
B.
C.
D.
E.

A. Match each picture with a description of the action(s). Write the correct letter on the line.

1. _____ blush (= turn red)

2. _____ hold hands (with)

3. _____ put one's arm (around)

4. _____ hug
   (= hold close to show affection—family and friends)

5. _____ embrace or hold someone in one's arms and kiss
   (= hold romantically to show love—couples)

B. Work in pairs. Cover the words. Look only at the pictures. Describe what each person is doing and why. (Make up your explanations.)

EXAMPLE: **Picture B**
   1. **What's she doing?** **She's hugging her grandmother.**
   2. **Why?** ...**because she loves her.**
      ...**because it's her birthday.**

C. In groups, talk about cultural differences. Answer these questions:

1. Do the young people in your culture show their feelings of friendship and affection the same way as in the pictures?

2. In your culture, do men and women act the same way when they are in love?

3. Do couples show affection in public in your culture?

4. How do parents express their love for their children?

Summarize your discussion for the class.

▦▦▦▦ EXPRESSIONS AND CONVERSATIONS

A. Practice the following conversation with your partner. Use the appropriate body language to act out (dramatize) the situation.

GIRL: Awww! <u>What a cute*</u> little puppy! Is it a male or female?

MAN: It's a female. Would you like to pet† her?

GIRL: May I? She <u>seems</u> very <u>obedient</u>. What's her name?

MAN: Her name is Lady. And you're right. She's very <u>good</u>. . .she never bites. That's a girl, Lady! Good dog!

B. Now practice the conversation again. Use different expressions for the underlined words. Have several different conversations.

EXAMPLE: [instead of] What a cute puppy!
[say] **Isn't that a darling puppy!**

▣ **Expressing Admiration**   (= expressing a positive opinion about a person or thing)

Awww!
Gee!
Gosh!
Wow!

What { **a cute*** / **an adorable** } puppy!
Isn't she (he) **a darling** little girl (boy)!
Isn't she (he, it) **cute!**

▣ **Making Compliments about Behavior**

Your puppy **seems obedient.**   She **is good.**
Your pet **behaves well.**   He **is an angel.**
Your dog **is** { **well-behaved.** / **well-trained.** }

---

*cute, darling, adorable (adj.) = pretty or handsome (said with affection)
†pet (v.) = touch an animal with the hand (with affection)

C. Practice the following conversation with your partner.

A: Gee, <u>you look pretty (handsome)</u> tonight!

B: Why, thank you. By the way, <u>you look very nice in that color.</u>
<u>It matches your eyes.</u> <u>Would you like</u> another drink?

A: No, thanks. <u>I</u> really <u>don't care for</u> anything.

B: Well, <u>how about</u> some cheese and crackers then?

Practice the conversation again. Use expressions from the following
list instead of the underlined words.

▣ Making Compliments about Appearance

You look $\begin{cases} \textbf{nice.} & \textit{(men and women)} \\ \textbf{great!} \end{cases}$

You look $\begin{cases} \textbf{beautiful.} & \textit{(women only)} \\ \textbf{pretty!} \end{cases}$

You look handsome! *(men only)*

That color **looks nice on** you!   It **matches** your eyes.
You **look nice in** that color!   It **goes with** your sweater.

▣ Offering Someone Something

Would you like some tea?   **How about** some coffee?
Can I get you something?   **What about** some dessert?
Do you want some more water?

▣ Refusing Something Politely

No, thank you. I don't care for anything.
No, thanks. I don't want any.

D. Practice the following conversation with your partner.

BOSS: Eleanor, sometimes I don't show it, but <u>I'm</u> really very <u>fond of you</u>.

SECRETARY: Well, <u>you are very nice</u> to me most of the time, and <u>I appreciate</u> that!

BOSS: In fact, I think <u>you're really terrific</u>, so I bought you this little present.

SECRETARY: Oh, <u>how nice of you</u>! You didn't have to do that...but, believe me, <u>I really appreciate</u> it!

Practice the conversation again. Use expressions from the following list instead of the underlined words.

🔲 **Expressing Affection**   (= telling someone how much you like or love him or her)

I'm fond of you.	You're really terrific!
I care for you.	You're a really special person!
You mean a lot to me.	

🔲 **Expressing Gratitude**   (= telling someone how much you appreciate his or her help, etc.)

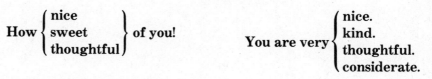

How { nice / sweet / thoughtful } of you!

You are very { nice. / kind. / thoughtful. / considerate. }

I really appreciate that!
I'm very grateful to you for that!

E. Now role play the situations in this section. Use your own words and the appropriate body language. How do you feel in each situation?

▧▧▧▧ EXPRESSING YOURSELF

What Do You Say? Use these expressions in your answers to the
questions that follow.

EXPRESSIONS

I really appreciate it.   How are you getting along?

Are you still in love?   Would you care for something else?

How considerate of you!   Did he ask you out yet?

I'm very fond of this place.   Will you marry me?

I'm very grateful for your help.

EXAMPLE: What do you say when you propose to someone?
        [say] **Will you marry me?**

WHAT DO YOU SAY?

1. ...when a guest is eating lunch at your home?

2. ...when someone sends you a card when you are sick?

3. ...when someone offers to help you with your homework?

4. ...when a female friend has a crush on someone?

5. ...when someone lends you some money?

6. ...when you return to your hometown?

7. ...when you meet a couple who have been married for fifty years?

8. ...when a friend calls you from his or her first job?

▨▨▨▨ ROLE PLAY

Work with a partner.
Choose one of the following situations.
Each student plays one role.
Read and think only about your role.
How do you feel?
Act out the situations. Use expressions from this chapter.
(Your teacher may ask a third student to direct and give suggestions.)

Role A	Role B
1. You are sitting on a bus. An older passenger gets on. You offer him or her your seat.	1. You are the older passenger. You are grateful to the younger person for offering you a seat.
2. You run into your neighbor at the grocery store. He or she has a new baby. You admire the baby.	2. You are the new parent. You accept the neighbor's compliments. You also describe how well-behaved your child is.
3. On your wedding anniversary, your married son or daughter gave you a surprise anniversary party. You call to thank him or her for being so considerate.	3. You accept your parent's thanks. You also explain that you are grateful to them for everything they did for you in the past.
4. You are attracted to someone at a party. You compliment the person on his or her appearance and ask if you can get him or her anything to eat or drink.	4. You are the other person at the party. You return the compliment but do not want anything else to eat or drink.
5. (your own situation) ?	5. (your own situation) ?

▧▧▧▧ INTERVIEW

Ask your partner the following questions. Take notes on the answers. (Your teacher may ask you to do this exercise in groups of three or four.)

1. Which person do you look up to the most in your family? In this country? In the world? Why do you admire him or her?

_____

EXAMPLE: [say] **In my family, I look up to my grandfather.**

_____

2. Are you a thoughtful person? Do you usually remember to send cards to friends and relatives on their birthdays and anniversaries?

3. Name several things you are thankful for in your life.

4. Are you affectionate with your family and friends? Is it acceptable for friends to be affectionate in public in your culture? What about couples?

5. Are you a romantic person? Name four romantic things people do when they fall in love.

6. What are the dating customs in your culture? Does an older person, a chaperone, go out with a young couple before they get married?

7. Do families sometimes arrange marriages for their children in your culture? At what age do most people marry? Is divorce acceptable in your culture?

Now change partners. Ask your new partner the same questions about his or her first partner. Use the third person, as in this example:

_____

EXAMPLE: Who does he look up to in his family?
       [say] **He looks up to his grandfather.**

_____

▧▧▧▧ ONE STEP FURTHER

GAME: "HOT SEAT"

You will need 3″ by 5″ cards for this game.

1. Write your name on a 3″ by 5″ card.

2. Write two questions about romance or friendship on the card. Use only the vocabulary from this chapter.

_____

EXAMPLE: [write] Did you go out with anyone last weekend? Have you ever been in love?

_____

3. Copy the same two questions in your notebook.

4. One student collects the cards.

5. Your teacher will select one student to sit in front of the class, in the "hot seat."

6. From the cards, your teacher will select individual students to ask their questions to the person in the "hot seat."

7. If a question is very personal, the person in the "hot seat" can say, "I pass."

8. If the student in the "hot seat" wants to, he or she can choose a famous movie star and pretend to be that person. (First, he or she should give the name of the movie star.)

9. The person in the "hot seat" must answer five questions before getting out of the "hot seat."

▨▨▨▨ PROBLEM SOLVING

Read the situation and possible solutions to yourself.
Which is the best solution? Write 1 next to the best idea, 2 next to the second best idea, and so forth.
Then work in groups of three or four. Choose a secretary.
Discuss your answers. Decide as a group the best order of the solutions.
The group secretary may write down the numbers.
Compare the answers of the different groups in the class.
Discuss why you chose certain solutions.

SITUATION: You are happily married except for one problem: your spouse (husband or wife) is jealous. He or she wants you to end your relationship with an old, close friend (of the opposite sex). You and your friend work together and you both like computers. You meet for lunch every few weeks. You are really *just friends*.

WHAT SHOULD YOU DO?

a. _____ Do what your spouse wants. Apologize to your old friend and explain that you can never meet again.

b. _____ Invite your friend to dinner and introduce your spouse to him or her. Reassure your spouse that your friendship is innocent.

c. _____ Your spouse is still suspicious even after meeting your friend. Suggest going to a marriage counselor.

d. _____ Your spouse refuses to go to a marriage counselor. Decide that he or she just doesn't trust you. Ask for a divorce.

e. _____ Stop seeing your old friend for a few months. Hope that your spouse will eventually change his or her mind.

f. _____ Have a serious discussion with your spouse. Explain that you feel insulted and leave for a few days. Wait for your spouse to apologize and ask you to come back.

g. _____ (your own solution)_____

_____

▦▦▦▦ WORDPLAY

A. **Prepositions.** Complete the story with the correct preposition. Use *to, with, for, of, in,* or *on.*

When I was your age, I was a tomboy. **I liked** __to__₁
play baseball and wear boys' clothes. I was very **fond** _____₂
fancy cars, too, especially convertibles. I never **cared** _____₃
party dresses.

When I was twelve and your father was sixteen, we were neighbors.
I helped him polish his convertible. I was very **nice** _____₄ him; I
brought him lemonade. And he was very **kind** _____₅ me. I
remember that he gave me his old car magazines. I guess that I **had a
crush** _____₆ him, but he didn't pay any attention to me because
I was so young.

Then my family moved away. When I returned to visit your father
a few years later, I was a grown-up young woman. I wasn't a tomboy
anymore! Of course, I **flirted** _____₇ him, and he **fell** _____₈
love _____₉ me. I remember we **went out** _____₁₀ **our first
date** in his convertible. After a few months, he **proposed** _____₁₁
me. Then we **got married** _____₁₂ each other. And that's the story
of our romance!

B. **Sentence Completion.** Make sentences from these words. Add
prepositions and other words you need. Use the past tense.

EXAMPLE: Rita / like / wear / boys' clothes
 [write] *Rita liked to wear boys' clothes.*

---

1. when / Rita / be / younger, / she / like to / play / baseball

_____

2. Rita / be / fond / cars, / but / do not care / party dresses

_____

3. she / admire / Bill / because / he / have / convertible

_____

4. she / look up / him, / and / he / be / nice / her

_____

5. when / she / grow up, / she / flirt / Bill

_____

6. Bill / ask / her / out / date, / and / they / fall / love

_____

7. after / they / got / married, / they / go / honeymoon

_____

C. **Parts of Speech**. Complete the story. Use the correct forms of the words.

People from all over the world come to see the unusual performances of trained dolphins and whales at Ocean World. The trainers* there have a very special relationship with these intelligent animals.

_____

friendship = noun   **friend** = noun   **friendly** = adjective

1. Twenty-three-year-old trainer Kim Harris has a warm
   <u>friendship</u> with the whales.

2. She is especially _____ with the oldest whale, Big Blue.

3. She gets along with him like a special _____ .

_____

*trainer (n.) = a person who teaches animals how to perform tricks

---

affection = noun   **affectionate** = adjective   **affectionately** = adverb

---

4. Kim is very _____ with Big Blue.

5. Kim likes to rub Blue's nose _____ , especially when he performs well.

6. Kim knows that Blue expects both fish and _____ as rewards†.

---

attraction = noun   **attractive** = adjective   **attract** = verb

---

7. Last week, Diva, a female dolphin, arrived at Ocean World. From the beginning, she paid attention only to Larry. Larry is an experienced trainer and a tall, _____ young man.

8. The other trainers discussed Diva's _____ to Larry. They decided that maybe she was in love.

9. "Oh, no," laughed Larry. "The bright colors of my bathing suit _____ her attention, not me!" he explained.

---

admiration = noun   **admire** = verb   **admiring** = adjective

---

10. During practice, you can feel the _____ of the trainers for the skill and intelligence of the dolphins.

11. When three dolphins jump together into the air, you have to _____ their perfect timing and grace.

12. The dolphins and whales all look proud when the _____ audiences clap for their exciting performances.

DISCUSSION (optional)

1. In your opinion, what qualities make a person able to train animals well?

2. Imagine you are a dolphin or whale. Would you enjoy your life performing for audiences at Ocean World? Why or why not?

3. Experiments show that dolphins communicate under water through sounds. In the future, do you think people will learn to talk to these intelligent animals?

---

†reward (n.) = gift for doing something well

CHAPTER 8

HATRED

▦▦▦▦ THE NEIGHBOR'S CAT

Look at the pictures and vocabulary words. Talk about what is happening in each picture.

1.

wake up / fence

2.

3.

4.

whistle / porch / handkerchief

5.

6.

confess*

7.

move out

8.

move in / noisy

---

*confess = admit

▓▓▓▓ WORDS AND EXPRESSIONS

expression	example
not get along with someone (= not have a good relationship)	*She doesn't get along with her roommate.*
dislike { someone or something + VERB*ing* (= not enjoy; not feel good about)	*I dislike that woman.* *I dislike taking examinations.*
can't stand someone or something (= not be able to tolerate)	*I can't stand listening to that song.*
be sick of + VERB*ing* (= be tired of)	*I'm sick of that singer.*
make someone **sick** *(slang)* (= cause strong dislike)	*I'm tired of him. In fact, he makes me sick.*
hate { someone or something + VERB*ing* **to** + VERB (= feel the opposite of love)	*I hate used car salespeople.* *I hate* { *buying* / *to buy* } *used cars.*
hurt someone's **feelings** (= make someone feel bad through words or actions)	*You hurt my feelings when you laughed at* *my pronunciation.*
be { **mean** / **cruel** } **to** someone (= be very unkind)	*The soldiers are very* { *mean* / *cruel* } *to the prisoners.*
avoid { someone or something + VERB*ing* (= keep away from someone or not do something)	*After our argument, I avoided him.* *He avoids taking taxis whenever he can.*
ignore someone or something (= not pay any attention to)	*When I asked my friend for a ride, she* *ignored me.*
hold a grudge against someone (= have a negative feeling about someone for a long time)	*After the argument, he held a grudge against his* *friend for two weeks.*
be jealous of someone or something (= a. want to get what someone else has b. not want to share a loved one with others)	*a. She's jealous* { *of him.* / *of his success.* } *b. I am jealous because he likes you.*
get revenge on someone **for** something *(very strong)* **get back at** someone **for** something (= do something bad to someone who has done something bad to you)	*His partner wanted to* { *get revenge on* / *get back at* } *him for* *his lies.*

expression	example
regret { something / + VERB*ing* (= feel bad about something you did in the past.	*She regrets* { *the decision.* / *quitting her job.*
forgive someone **for** { something / + VERB*ing* (= no longer feel angry about something)	*After I explained the situation,* / *my friend forgave me for* { *my late arrival.* / *arriving late.*

▧▧▧▧ TELLING THE STORY

A. Look at the picture story. Underline the correct word(s) to complete each sentence.

EXAMPLE: The man (likes / <u>dislikes</u>) cats.

1. He calls the Animal Control Center because he (can't stand / loves) the neighbor's cat.
2. At first, the man (ignores / pays attention to) the neighbor's feelings about her missing cat.
3. The wife tells her husband that he was (kind / mean) to the neighbor.
4. The man (avoids / doesn't avoid) telling the neighbor about her cat.
5. The neighbor moves because she (can't forgive / forgives) the man.
6. When she moves out, the neighbor (gets back / doesn't get back) at the man next door.
7. When the husband sees the new neighbors, he (doesn't regret / regrets) calling the Animal Control Center.

B. How well did you understand the story? Don't look at the pictures. Write **T** if the statement is **true**, **F** if it is **false**.

EXAMPLE: _F_ The man hated cats because he was allergic to them.

1. _____ He couldn't stand the neighbor's cat because it woke him up.
2. _____ His wife disliked the neighbor because she was mean to her cat.
3. _____ At first, the man ignored the neighbor's feelings.
4. _____ When the man finally talked to the neighbor, he avoided looking at her because he couldn't see.

5. _____ The man hurt the neighbor's feelings.

6. _____ The neighbor immediately forgave the man.

7. _____ In the end, the neighbor got back at the man for his actions.

8. _____ When the new neighbors moved in, the husband regretted calling the Animal Control Center.

C. Work with a partner. Explain or correct the false statements.

EXAMPLE: [say] **The example is false. He hated cats because they make a lot of noise.**

⬛⬛⬛⬛ BODY LANGUAGE

A. Match each picture with a description of the action. Write the correct letter on the line.

1. _____ stare (at)
(= look at for a long time)

2. _____ look away or look the other way

3. _____ turn up one's nose (at)
(= show dislike or a feeling of superiority)

4. _____ stick out one's tongue (at) *(children only)*

5. _____ turn thumbs down

6. _____ hiss and boo
(= yell words of dislike)

B. Work in pairs. Cover the words. Look only at the pictures. Describe what each person is doing and why. (Make up your explanations.)

EXAMPLE: **Picture D**
   1. **What's he doing?   He's staring.**
   2. **Why?   . . .because he can't stand people with long hair.**
          . . .because he hates that kind of food.

C. In groups, talk about cultural differences. Answer these questions:

1. Do the people in your culture show their feelings of dislike in the same way as in the pictures?

2. Do men in your culture show dislike in the same way as women?

3. In what other ways do you express dislike or jealousy?

Summarize your discussion for the class.

▨▨▨▨ EXPRESSIONS AND CONVERSATIONS

A. Practice the following conversation with your partner. Use the appropriate body language to act out (dramatize) the situation.

JOE: Sam, I <u>don't want to face it</u> but I have to go to the dentist when we get home.

SAM: I know what you mean! I <u>can't stand</u> going to the dentist. I always avoid going.

JOE: I <u>avoided</u> it for years, too. But now I have a toothache.

SAM: That's too bad. A visit to the dentist is worse than a month in space!

JOE: Believe me, I'm <u>not looking forward to</u> it.

B. Now practice the conversation again. Use different expressions for the underlined words. Have several different conversations.

EXAMPLE: [instead of] I don't want to face it.
                  [say] **I don't want to think about it.**

▨ **Expressing Dislike**

I $\left\{ \begin{array}{l} \textbf{can't stand} \\ \textbf{can't bear} \\ \textbf{hate} \end{array} \right\}$ going to the dentist.
to go to the dentist

▨ **Expressing Dread**   (= expressing dislike about something you have to do)

I'm $\left\{ \begin{array}{l} \textbf{not looking forward to} \\ \textbf{dreading} \end{array} \right\}$ my dentist appointment.

▨ **Avoiding or Ignoring Something**   (= not paying attention to something)

I $\left\{ \begin{array}{l} \textbf{don't want to face} \text{ it.} \\ \textbf{don't want to think about} \text{ it.} \end{array} \right.$

I $\left\{ \begin{array}{l} \textbf{avoid} \text{ it.} \\ \textbf{put it off.} \end{array} \right.$

C. Practice the following conversation with your partner.

SUSIE: I <u>hate</u> you! You pulled my hair!

FATHER: Children, <u>behave yourselves!</u> Do you hear? <u>Stop fighting!</u>

KATIE: Daddy, she's <u>being mean to</u> me! Tell her to stop.

FATHER: Now <u>don't be naughty</u>, children...or I'll spank both of you! Do you understand?

Practice the conversation again. Use expressions from the following list instead of the underlined words.

▣ Complaining *(usually by children)*

I **hate** you!　　　　　　　She's **(being) mean to** me.
I **can't stand** you!　　　　She's **not nice to** me.

▣ Scolding or Correcting Children

Don't be naughty!　　　　**Behave** yourselves!
Don't misbehave!　　　　**Be good!**
　　　　　　　　　　　　　Act like good children (girls) (boys)!

Stop fighting.
Quit causing trouble.

D. Practice the following conversation with your partner.

HUSBAND: Oh, no! A letter about the cat from the neighbor. Boy, <u>I regret doing</u> that now.

WIFE: Well, you <u>made a big mistake</u>, and now you have to pay for it.

HUSBAND: Believe me, <u>I will never do</u> that <u>again</u>.

WIFE: But you already hurt her feelings. Pets are very important to old people. You really were <u>very mean</u> to her.

Practice the conversation again. Use expressions from the following list instead of the underlined words.

⊠ **Criticizing**   (= telling someone you don't approve of his or her behavior)

You { made a big mistake.
      did the wrong thing. }

You were **very** { **mean**
                     cruel } to her.

⊠ **Expressing Regret**   (= feeling bad about something that you did)

I regret doing
I'm sorry that I did } that.

I will never do
I'm never going to do } that **again**.

E. Now role play the situations in this section. Use your own words and the appropriate body language. How do you feel in each situation?

⊠⊠⊠⊠ EXPRESSING YOURSELF

A. **What Do You Say?** Use these expressions in your answers to the questions that follow.

EXPRESSIONS

We don't get along.

I can't stand it any more.

You hurt my feelings.

I don't like to hold grudges.

I'll get even with you!

I really regret that.

Please forgive me!

Why are you ignoring me?

I'm jealous.

EXAMPLE: What do you say when you do something wrong?
         [say] **Please forgive me!**

WHAT DO YOU SAY?

1. . . . when someone asks you why you never speak to your neighbor?

2. . . . when you make a mistake that causes many problems?

3. . . . when you finally decide to leave a very unpleasant job?

4. . . . when a friend buys a beautiful new car?

5. . . . when a friend asks you why you're friendly with a person who hurt you in the past?

6. . . . when someone acts very unfairly toward you?

7. . . . when someone says something unkind to you?

8. . . . when a friend doesn't pay attention to you at a party?

B. **How Do You Act or Feel?** Work with your partner. Take turns asking and answering the following questions. Answer in complete sentences, using *when* and the vocabulary below. (Many of the questions require the word *it*.) Use each answer only once.

hate	complain
ignore	avoid
dislike	not like
get jealous	regret

SITUATION: You make a bad decision.

EXAMPLE: [ask]How do you act or feel when you make a bad decision?
[answer]**When I make a bad decision, I regret it.**

SITUATIONS

1. Your girlfriend or boyfriend goes out with another person.

2. The waitress serves you cold tea in a restaurant.

3. You don't want to go to the dentist.

4. The person behind you is talking loudly in the movie theater.

5. You buy something that doesn't work.

6. A stranger* writes you a letter asking for $100.

7. You have to wait in line for half an hour at the bank.

---

*stranger (n.) = someone you don't know

▨▨▨▨ ROLE PLAY

Work with a partner.
Choose one of the following situations.
Each student plays one role.
Read and think only about your role.
How do you feel?
Act out the situations. Use expressions from this chapter.
(Your teacher may ask a third student to direct and give suggestions.)

Role A	Role B
1. You explain to your roommate that all your clothes are dirty and you have to go to the laundromat. You're not looking forward to that.	1. You understand your roommate's feelings because you hate going to the laundromat, too. You tell your roommate some of the other things you hate to do.
2. You are babysitting for two children who aren't behaving well. You scold them.	2. You are a naughty child. You refuse to finish your ice cream because your brother ate some of it.
3. You call up one of your classmates to invite him or her to go with you to a horror movie.	3. When a classmate invites you to go to a horror movie, you decline (say no to) the invitation. You explain that you hate horror films because they give you nightmares.
4. You are the manager of a restaurant. Your best chef* just quit because you made fun of his foreign accent several times. You explain that you were not serious, and regret your comments.	4. You are the owner of the restaurant. You explain to the manager that it was a big mistake to make fun of the chef and that he was an excellent cook. You criticize the manager.
5. (your own situation) ?	5. (your own situation) ?

*chef (n.) = the cook in a hotel or large restaurant

▨▨▨▨. INTERVIEW

Ask your partner the following questions. Take notes on the answers.

1. When you get a parking ticket, do you usually ignore it or pay it?

_____

EXAMPLE: [say] **When I get a parking ticket, I usually pay it.**

_____

2. What was the last thing you avoided doing? Who was the last person you avoided seeing?

3. Is there anything in your life that you really regret doing? If you are from another country, do you ever regret leaving your country and moving? Why?

4. Are little children sometimes cruel to each other? To animals? In your opinion, why?

5. Have you ever been jealous of someone? Why were you jealous? How did you act?

6. If a child misbehaves (acts badly), should an adult spank him or her? If not, what should an adult do? Did your parents spank you when you were a child?

7. Name a famous person that you can't stand. What don't you like about him or her? Is there anything about your country or the country you live in now that you can't stand?

8. *Hate* is the opposite of *love*. In your opinion, which emotion is stronger, hate or love? Why?

Now change partners. Ask your new partner the same questions about his or her first partner. Use the third person, as in this example:

_____

EXAMPLE: What does he do when he gets a parking ticket?
  [say] **When he gets a parking ticket, he usually pays it.**

_____

▨▨▨▨ ONE STEP FURTHER

GAME: "GUESS WHO"

You will need 3″ by 5″ cards for this game.

1. On one side of the card, write *three* things you love, or really like, about the country you are living in now or your own country.

_____

EXAMPLE: [write] 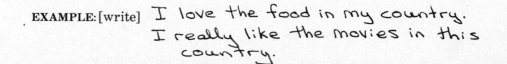 I love the food in my country.
I really like the movies in this country.

_____

2. On the other side, write *three* things you hate, or really dislike, about the country you are living in or your own country.

3. Do not write your name on the card.

4. Do not show your answers to anyone.

5. One student will collect the cards.

6. The teacher will read the cards aloud.

7. The students will try to guess who wrote each card.

8. After five wrong guesses, the student who wrote the card must identify himself or herself.

▨▨▨▨ PROBLEM SOLVING

Read the situation and possible solutions to yourself.
Which is the best solution? Write 1 next to the best idea, 2 next to the second best idea, and so forth.
Then work in groups of three or four. Choose a secretary.
Discuss your answers. Decide as a group the best order of the solutions.
The group secretary may write down the numbers.
Compare the answers of the different groups in the class.
Discuss why you chose certain solutions.

SITUATION: Your new job in an office is fine except for one thing: three workers in the same room with you smoke all day. You begin to feel very sick and think maybe you are allergic* to cigarette smoke.

WHAT SHOULD YOU DO?

a. _____ Don't explain why you feel sick to anyone. Quit your job and start looking for another job.

b. _____ Don't complain to the manager. Buy an expensive air-cleaning machine and use it every day.

c. _____ Ask your fellow workers to stop smoking in the office. Ask them to smoke outside during their breaks instead.

d. _____ If your fellow workers refuse to stop smoking in the office, explain the problem to the manager. Report the situation to the health department if the manager doesn't solve the problem in two weeks.

e. _____ Give a doctor's letter proving your allergy to cigarette smoke to a lawyer. Stay home from work and collect sick pay until the lawyer solves the problem with the manager.

f. _____ (your own solution)_____

_____

_____

---

*allergic (adj.) = very sensitive to something

▨▨▨▨ WORDPLAY

A. **Prepositions.** Complete these New Year's resolutions with the correct prepositions. Use *at, to, with, of, on, against,* or *for.*

January 1st

New Year's Resolutions

Dear Diary,

This year I promise . . .

1. At school, I will try to **get along** _____with_____ all my teachers.

2. When I am **sick** _____ homework, I won't complain anymore.

3. At home, I won't be **mean** _____ my younger brother, Teddy.

4. I will never be **jealous** _____ my popular older sister, Sara, again.

5. I won't try to **get back** _____ Teddy _____ his tricks.

6. I will **forgive** my parents _____ everything.

7. I will never try to **get revenge** _____ anyone, especially Sara, again.

8. I won't **hold a grudge** _____ Sara, either.

Jessica

B. **Sentence Completion.** Make sentences from these words. Add prepositions and other words you need. Use the past or past continuous tense, as appropriate.

_____

EXAMPLE: do / man's / wife / get along / neighbor / ? yes / she / do

[write] Did the man's wife get along with the neighbor? Yes, she did.

_____

1. man / can't stand / cat / because / it / wake / him / up

_____

2. when / he / call / Animal Control Center, / he / be / cruel / neighbor

_____

3. wife / feel sorry / for / neighbor / because / husband / hurt / her / feelings

_____

4. do / neighbor / forgive / him / ?   no / she / do not

_____

5. how / do / she / get back / him?

_____

6. she / move away / and / rent / house / to / noisy / neighbors

_____

7. do / husband / regret / calling / Animal Control Center / ?   yes / he / do

_____

C. **Parts of Speech**. Complete the story about Cinderella. Use the correct forms of the words.

Traditional stories for children are called _fairy tales._ "Cinderella," like other famous fairy tales, contains many negative emotions, such as hatred and jealousy.

_____

hatred = noun   **hate** = verb   **hatefully** = adverb

_____

1. Cinderella ___hated___ working from morning till night.

2. Her two ugly stepsisters spoke _____ about Cinderella because she was so young and beautiful.

3. Sometimes, she could see the _____ in their eyes.

---

cruelty = noun   **cruel** = adjective   **cruelly** = adverb

---

4. The two sisters often treated Cinderella very _____ .

5. She tried to ignore them when they were _____ to her.

6. Because of their _____ , Cinderella was very unhappy.

---

jealousy = noun   **jealous** = adjective   **jealously** = adverb

---

7. The sisters were _____ of Cinderella's youth and beauty.

8. When they saw Cinderella in a beautiful dress at the dance, they could not hide their _____ .

9. The two sisters stared _____ at Cinderella while she danced with the prince.

DISCUSSION (optional)

1. Name some popular fairy tales from your culture.

2. Does it hurt children to hear stories about jealousy and cruelty, like "Cinderella," or does it prepare them for "real life"?

CHAPTER 9

BELIEF

▨▨▨▨ THE WINNING CANDIDATE

Look at the pictures and vocabulary words. Talk about what is happening in each picture.

1.

vote*

2.

3.

safe / keys

4.

candidate†

5.

6.

make a speech

7.

debate††

8.

election‡

---

*vote (v.) = choose a person to hold an office
†candidate (n.) = person who seeks an office
††debate (n.) = a formal discussion of different points of view
‡election (n.) = process of voting

▨▨▨▨ WORDS AND EXPRESSIONS

expression	example
be { **sure** / **certain** } { **of** something / **about** something / **that** + SUBJECT + VERB } (= feel strongly that something is true)	I'm { *sure* / *certain* } { *of that fact.* / *about the answer to that question.* / *that you are right.* }
be **confident** { **of** something / **about** { something / + VERB*ing* } } (= believe in or feel sure about something)	*The applicant is very confident* { *of his ability.* / *about the exam.* / *about getting the job.* }
believe someone (= feel that what someone says is true)	*He didn't believe me when I told him my age.*
believe in someone or something (= feel that someone is dependable)	*My parents believe in me.*
believe { **in** + VERB*ing* / **that** + SUBJECT + VERB } (= feel that something is right or true)	*She believes in working for peace.* *I believe that all people are created equal.*
trust someone **with** something **have trust in** someone or something (= believe someone or something is honest and dependable)	*I trust you with the money.* *I have trust in the laws of our country.*
have faith / **have confidence** } **in** someone or something (= be sure of or trust someone's abilities or intentions)	*I have faith in the president.* *I have confidence in your work.*
rely / **depend** / **count** } **on** someone { **for** something / **to** + VERB } (= feel sure about)	*I rely on my family for support.* *You can { depend / count } on me to help you.*
be { **dependable** / **reliable** / **responsible** / **trustworthy** }	*She is a very* { *dependable* / *reliable* / *responsible* / *trustworthy* } *employee. The boss trusts her.*
tell (someone) **the truth** **be honest with** someone **about** something (= not to lie)	*He's telling you the truth about the money.* *He's being honest with you about the money.*
be { **frank** / **sincere** } { **with** someone **about** something / **about** something } (= be open and honest)	*She was very frank with me about the problem.* *I think he's very sincere about his apology.*

expression	example
make a promise } { **to** + VERB **promise** } { **that** + SUBJECT + VERB (= say that you will definitely do something)	He *made a promise* } { *to give back the money.* *promises* } { *that he will give back the money.*
swear to someone **that** + SUBJECT + VERB (= make a serious promise that something is true or that you will do something)	*He swore to me that he was telling the truth.* *She swears that she will never steal anything again.*
convince someone **to** + VERB (= influence someone to make a decision)	*He convinced me to get married.*
make up one's **mind to** + VERB (= make a decision)	*She made up her mind to quit her job.*
be { **gullible** { **naive** (= believe everything you see or hear)	*Susan is very* { *gullible.* { *naive.* *She believes everything she reads in the newspaper.*
be a sucker *(slang)* (= believe anything)	*You were a sucker to believe that advertisement.*

▨▨▨▨ TELLING THE STORY

A. Look at the picture story. Underline the correct word(s) to complete each sentence.

EXAMPLE: The students think that they (<u>can rely on</u> / can't depend on) Carmen to be a good treasurer.*

---

1. Carmen stays in the office late to finish her work because she is a very (responsible / irresponsible) employee.

2. Her boss (trusts / doesn't trust) her with the keys to the safe.

3. When the old politician convinces Carmen to become a candidate, she (makes up / doesn't make up) her mind to run for office.

4. She is (certain / uncertain) that she can beat the other candidate, Biggs.

5. During her campaign, Carmen (promises / doesn't promise) to do certain things if she is elected.

6. During the debate, Biggs says that he (believes / doesn't believe) what she says.

---

*treasurer (n.) = person responsible for money

B. How well did you understand the story? Don't look at the pictures. Write **T** if the statement is **true**, **F** if it is **false**.

EXAMPLE: __F__ The students who vote for Carmen depend on her to be a dishonest treasurer.

---

1. _____ At work, she is a very reliable employee.
2. _____ The boss doesn't trust her with the keys to the safe.
3. _____ The experienced politician convinces her to run for office.
4. _____ Carmen isn't sure that she can beat the other candidate, Biggs.
5. _____ She promises certain things to the public during the campaign.
6. _____ Biggs believes that she is telling the truth.
7. _____ A lot of voters have confidence in her.

C. Work with a partner. Explain or correct the false statements.

EXAMPLE: [say] **The example is not true. She got an award for being honest.**

▨▨▨▨ BODY LANGUAGE

A. Match each picture with a description of the action. Write the correct letter on the line.

A.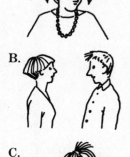

1. _____ look someone straight in the eye

2. _____ give someone the "okay" sign

B.

3. _____ nod one's head (in agreement)

4. _____ shake hands (with someone) (in agreement)

5. _____ keep one's fingers crossed
   (= gesture made when you hope something good will happen)

C.

B. Work in pairs. Cover the words. Look only at the pictures. Describe what each person is doing and why. (Make up your explanations.)

D.

EXAMPLE: Picture B
1. **What's she doing?** She's looking him straight in the eye.
2. **Why?** ...because she's telling him the truth.
   ...because she's being honest with him.

E.

C. In groups, talk about cultural differences. Answer these questions:

1. Do people in your culture act in the same way as in the pictures:

   a. when they believe something is "okay"?

   b. when they make an agreement?

   c. when they hope that something good will happen?

2. In what other ways do you express belief or certainty in your culture?

Summarize your discussion for the class.

▨▨▨▨ EXPRESSIONS AND CONVERSATIONS

A. Practice the following conversation with your partner. Use the appropriate body language to act out (dramatize) the situation.

GRANDPARENT: I'm afraid <u>I don't have confidence in</u> young people any more...

TEENAGER: Why do you say that? Kids today aren't very different from kids when you were growing up, are they? They're pretty reliable, I think.

GRANDPARENT: Dear, the problem is teenagers don't believe in working hard any more! <u>You</u> just <u>can't rely on</u> them.

TEENAGER: <u>Are you kidding?</u> <u>That's not true!</u> Maybe some are like that, but certainly not all.

B. Now practice the conversation again. Use different expressions for the underlined words. Have several different conversations.

EXAMPLE: [instead of] I don't have confidence in young people any more.
[say] **I don't have faith in young people any more.**

▨ **Expressing Loss of Confidence**   (= expressing loss of a stong belief in someone or something)

I don't $\begin{Bmatrix} \text{have confidence in} \\ \text{have faith in} \end{Bmatrix}$ young people (politicians, our leaders, etc.).

You can't $\begin{Bmatrix} \text{rely on} \\ \text{depend on} \end{Bmatrix}$ them.

▨ **Expressing Disbelief**   (= expressing a lack of belief)

That's not true!
That's ridiculous!

Are you $\begin{Bmatrix} \text{kidding?} \\ \text{joking?} \end{Bmatrix}$
Are you serious?

C. Practice the following conversation with your partner.

A: Do you believe in life after death?

B: <u>I'm not sure</u>. I don't think about it very much, I guess. But <u>it's hard to believe</u> that *this* is all there is...

A: Well, <u>I'm sure about</u> one thing. We are all going to die one day! *(They both laugh.)*

B: Oh, <u>without a doubt!</u> You are right about that!

A: *(laughing)* <u>You can count on</u> only two things in life, you know: death and taxes!

Practice the conversation again. Use expressions from the following list instead of the underlined words.

▦ Expressing Certainty

I'm $\begin{Bmatrix} \text{sure} \\ \text{certain} \\ \text{positive} \end{Bmatrix}$ about...   Without a doubt,...
No doubt about it,...
Absolutely!

You can count on that.
You can depend on that.

▦ Expressing Uncertainty

I'm not $\begin{Bmatrix} \text{sure.} \\ \text{certain.} \\ \text{positive.} \end{Bmatrix}$ It's hard to believe...
It's difficult to imagine...
I don't know.

D. Practice the following conversation with your partner.

MAN: I don't know. It's not a bad price, but maybe I shouldn't buy it.

WOMAN: Look, why don't you make up your mind! It's getting late, and I'm exhausted.

MAN: It's a pretty good deal, but I can't decide about the color. What do you think?

WOMAN: It's hard to say which color is better, but you can't beat the price! Just choose one, please, and let's go home!

Practice the conversation again. Use expressions from the following list instead of the underlined words.

▣ **Expressing Indecision**   (= saying that you can't decide)

I'm not sure.
I don't know.
It's hard to say.

I can't { decide.
make a decision.
make up my mind.

▣ **Convincing Someone of Something**

It's **not a bad** price!   You **can't beat the** price!
It's **a good** deal!   I **won't find a better** deal!

E. Now role play the situations in this section. Use your own words and the appropriate body language. How do you feel in each situation?

▧▧▧▧ EXPRESSING YOURSELF

A. **What Do You Say?** Use these expressions in your answers to the questions that follow.

EXPRESSIONS

I'll be frank with you.

Have confidence in yourself!

I can't make up my mind.

You're so naive...

(Do you) Promise not to tell anyone?

Don't be such a sucker!

Sounds too good to be true.

Can I count on you?

I swear I didn't do it.

EXAMPLE: What do you say when someone promises you something unbelievable or fantastic.
[say] **Sounds too good to be true.**

WHAT DO YOU SAY?

1. ...when a friend thinks the diamond she bought for five dollars is real?

2. ...when you need someone to help you with something?

3. ...when you want to tell a very important secret to someone?

4. ...when two people ask you to go out on the same evening?

5. ...when someone doesn't believe he or she can improve his or her life?

6. ...when you have to tell someone something negative or critical?

7. ...when a friend believes that if she takes a certain pill, she can eat ice cream every day and still lose weight?

8. ...when someone says that you broke or took something that you didn't?

B. **What Do You Believe In?** Work with your partner. Take turns asking and answering the following questions. Answer in complete sentences.

EXAMPLE: ghosts (= the spirits of dead people)
           [ask] **Do you believe in ghosts?**
           [answer] **No, I don't believe in ghosts.** [or] **Yes, I believe in ghosts.**

---

1. superstitions (= common beliefs not based on science or reason)
   Ex: *Some people believe that if you break a mirror, you will have seven years of bad luck.*

2. magic (= the ability to do unusual or unbelievable things through special powers)
   Ex: *Some people believe that magicians (people who practice magic) can make objects disappear.*

3. witches (= women with supernatural or special powers)
   Ex: *Some people believe that witches can make sick people better without medicine.*

4. extraterrestrials (= beings from other planets)
   Ex: *E.T. is a famous movie about an extraterrestrial who visits earth.*

5. miracles (= strange events that seem to be caused by a higher power)
   Ex: *When a very ill person suddenly recovers, some people believe that a miracle has happened.*

6. heaven (= place where very good people go after they die)
   Ex: *Some people believe that if you always help people during your life, you will probably go to heaven when you die.*

7. hell (= place where very bad people go after they die)
   Ex: *Some people believe that if you kill another person, you will probably go to hell when you die.*

8. reincarnation (= rebirth in a new form after death)
   Ex: *Some people believe they were animals in their past lives.*

GROUP DISCUSSION (optional)

1. Why do (or don't) you believe in these ideas or things?

2. In your culture, which of these ideas do most people believe in?

3. Which religions believe in the last four ideas?

▨▨▨▨ ROLE PLAY

Work with a partner.
Choose one of the following situations.
Each student plays one role.
Read and think only about your role.
How do you feel?
Act out the situations. Use expressions from this chapter.
(Your teacher may ask a third student to direct and give suggestions.)

Role A	Role B
1. You can't make up your mind about your vacation. It's cheaper to go camping in the mountains, but you prefer the beach. Explain your indecision to the friend you are going with.	1. You are not sure which vacation is better, but you want your friend to make reservations today, before it's too late.
2. You are taking a phone survey* about the next election. You want to know if people still have faith in the president and their reasons why or why not.	2. You are a typical citizen. You must answer questions about the president *honestly*. Do you trust him? Why or why not?
3. Your car won't start, and you're looking for a reliable mechanic. Describe to your friend some bad experiences with mechanics in the past.	3. You recommend your mechanic to your friend because you trust him and you think he is very honest and dependable.
4. You are absolutely sure that you saw a UFO† in the sky while you were driving home from work. You tell your roommate about it.	4. You don't believe that your roommate saw a UFO and you try to convince him or her that it was an airplane instead.
5. (your own situation) ?	5. (your own situation) ?

---

*survey (n.) = questions to learn opinions on a specific topic
†UFO (n.) = Unidentified Flying Object = unknown thing in the sky

❖❖❖❖ INTERVIEW

Ask your partner the following questions. Take notes on the answers. (Your teacher may ask you to do this exercise in groups of three or four.)

1. In your opinion, are American cars or foreign cars more dependable? Why?

_____

EXAMPLE: [say] **I think Japanese cars are more dependable because you don't have to repair them often.**

_____

2. Do you believe everything you read in the newspaper, hear on the radio, and see on TV? What kinds of things do you *not* believe? Give examples.

3. During our lives, we have to trust certain professionals, like bankers, with things we own...and sometimes even our lives. Name five other kinds of professionals we have to trust.

4. What person(s) do you depend on the most in your life for help and advice? Does anyone depend on you?

5. In your native country, can you rely on the post office to deliver important or valuable mail on time? What about in the country you live in now?

6. "Honesty is the best policy" is a saying in English. What does that mean? Do you have a similar saying in your language? Explain.

Now change partners. Ask your new partner the same questions about his or her first partner. Use the third person, as in this example:

_____

EXAMPLE: What kind of car does she think is the most dependable?
       [say] **She thinks Japanese cars are the most dependable because you don't have to repair them often.**

_____

❖❖❖❖ ONE STEP FURTHER

GAME: "LIE DETECTOR"

For this game, you will need 3″ by 5″ cards.

1. Write six statements about yourself on a 3″ x 5″ card. Three statements must be true, and three must be false. Mix up the order of the true and false statements. Here are some things you can write about:

EXAMPLE: name, age, weight, height, present occupation, name of your native country, number of brothers and sisters, kind of job in your native country, what you had for dinner last night, your favorite food, music, movie star, etc.

---

2. Exchange your card with your partner. Do not talk to each other.

3. You must guess which statements about your partner are true and which are false. Write an X in front of the false statements.

4. Return the card to your partner.

5. Discuss the right and wrong answers with your partner. Did anyone get a perfect score? How did he or she know the truth?

▨▨▨▨ PROBLEM SOLVING

Read the situation and possible solutions to yourself.
Which is the best solution? Write 1 next to the best idea, 2 next to the second best idea, and so forth.
Then work in groups of three or four.
Choose a secretary for your group.
Discuss your answers. Decide as a group the best order of the solutions.
The group secretary may write down the numbers.
Compare the answers of the different groups in the class.
Discuss why you chose certain solutions.

SITUATION: There is going to be a talent show at our school. All your friends have encouraged you to sing in the show, but you are very shy and afraid to sing in public.

WHAT SHOULD YOU DO?

a. _____ Be honest with yourself and admit that you're not ready. Decide to wait until you have more confidence in your singing.

b. _____ Don't let your friends down. Make up your mind to perform even if you're very nervous. Have faith in yourself and do your best.

c. _____ Be frank with your friends. Tell them that you appreciate their enthusiasm. Explain that you are so shy that you will never sing in public.

d. _____ Force yourself to perform, even though you are very nervous and sick before the curtain opens. Faint on the stage.

e. _____ Convince your friends that you intend to perform. Then pretend to get sick on the day of the talent show and don't perform.

f. _____ (your own solution)_____

_____

_____

▨▨▨▨ WORDPLAY

A. **Prepositions.** Complete the story with the correct prepositions. Use *to, about, with, for, in,* or *on.*

FEDERAL PRISON*
Jackson, Mississippi
October 10

Dear Mother,

There is only one thing I'm **certain** ___about___₁ any more. You are the only person who can help me now. You are the only person who **believes** _____₂ me. Mother, I am **depending** _____₃ you _____₄ help. Please don't let me down!

I'm going to be **honest** _____₅ you, Mom. You are the only person who can prove that I am innocent† in court. Can I **rely** _____₆ you to help me at the trial††? Can I **count** _____₇ you to prove that I am innocent?

My lawyer **convinced** me _____₈ write you to ask for your help. I know sometimes we don't get along very well, but I really need you right now. I am not an angel but, believe me, Mom, I didn't do anything wrong.

Love,

Dean

---

*prison (n.) = jail
†innocent (adj.) = not responsible for a crime
††trial (n.) = determining guilt or innocence

B. **Sentence Completion**. Make sentences from these words. Add prepositions and other words you need. Use the past or past continuous tense, as appropriate.

EXAMPLE: students / vote / Carmen / because / they / can / depend / her

[write] *The students voted for Carmen because they could depend on her.*

1. Carmen / be / more / reliable / than / other / employees

2. why / do / boss / trust / her / keys / ?

3. do / politican / convince / her / become a candidate / ?

4. Carmen / be / confident / that / she / can / beat / Biggs

5. she / make / promises / voters

6. Biggs / not believe / Carmen's / promises

7. voters / vote / Carmen / because / they / have / faith / her

C. **Parts of Speech**. Complete the story. Use the correct forms of the words.

Each year, many airplane pilots report UFOs (Unidentified Flying Objects) in the sky. How many of these reports are true? Who can we believe?

OPINION PAGE

belief = noun	**unbelievable** = adjective	**believe** = verb

1. Do you __believe__ in UFOs?

2. Every day hundreds of people tell _____ stories about UFOs to news reporters and government officials all over America.

3. Other people make fun of them for their _____ in these strange objects.

---

truth = noun **true** = adjective **truthfully** = adverb

---

4. It is possible that some people make up* stories about UFOs that aren't _____ .

5. But when airline pilots report UFOs, I believe they are telling the _____ .

6. I also believe that some military pilots have _____ reported seeing UFOs.

---

certainty = noun **uncertain** = adjective **certainly** = adverb

---

7. Why are people _____ about the honesty of pilots who report UFOs?

8. These pilots _____ must try to tell the truth.

9. Why do people question the _____ of their reports?

---

honesty = noun **honest** = adjective **honestly** = adverb

---

10. I _____ believe that the public is afraid of the truth about UFOs.

11. Why should we question the _____ of commercial and military pilots who report UFOs?

12. What this country needs is an _____ government investigation into these UFO reports!

DISCUSSION (optional)

1. Do you believe that earth is the only planet in the universe where intelligent life exists?

2. Have you (or has anyone you know) ever seen a UFO? If you are from another country, are there UFO reports in the newspapers in your country?

3. If beings from other planets visit the earth in the future, will they look like us? Will they be peaceful?

4. Do you enjoy science fiction books and movies? Which one is your favorite?

---

*make up (v.) = invent

DOUBT

❂❂❂❂ WHO CAN YOU TRUST?

Look at the pictures and vocabulary words. Talk about what is
happening in each picture.

1.

gangster / jewelry store

2.

salesperson / diamond ring

3.

one-hundred-dollar bill

4.

jeweler / magnifying glass

5.

examine

6.

7.

8.

✚✚✚✚ WORDS AND EXPRESSIONS

expression	example
wonder { **about** someone or something / **if** / **whether** } + SUBJECT + VERB (= ask oneself)	*I wonder about this gift.* *I wonder { if / whether } I can return it.*
be { **unsure** / **uncertain** } **about** something (= not know for a fact)	*I'm unsure about what time the class starts.* *She's uncertain about his age.*
doubt { someone or something / **that** / **if** / **whether** } + SUBJECT + VERB (= be uncertain about)	*I doubt him (his honesty).* *I doubt { that / if / whether } he's telling the truth.*
suspect someone **of** { + VERB*ing* / something } **be suspicious of** someone (= believe someone has done or may do something wrong)	*The police suspect him of { stealing the bike. / the crime. }* *I am suspicious of him because he looks dishonest.*
distrust someone or something (= lack faith or confidence)	*I distrust the information in that report.*
be dishonest with someone **about** something (= tell a lie or deceive)	*He was dishonest with me about his feelings.*
lie to someone **about** { + VERB*ing* / something } **tell** someone **a lie** (= not to tell the truth)	*She lied to me about { going to the party. / the money. }* *She told me a lie about her age.*
be a liar (= not speak the truth)	*The politician shouted, "He is a liar! I don't believe a word he says!"*
be a { **criminal** / **gangster** / **thief** / **crook** / **con man** } (= be a person who breaks the law or cheats someone)	*Don't buy anything from him; he's a criminal.*
be { **(a) fake** / **counterfeit** (*usually money*) } (= be a copy; not be real)	*That painting is a fake.* *He made counterfeit money in his basement.*

expression	example
cheat { someone **out of** something **at** (a game) **on** (a test, taxes, etc.) (= a. take from someone unfairly b. play a game dishonestly c. do something dishonestly)	*a. The salesman cheated me out of my money.* *b. He cheated at cards and won.* *c. He cheated on the test, but he still didn't pass it.*
rip someone **off** *(slang)* (= cheat someone)	*That salesman ripped me off. I want a refund.*
be a rip-off *(slang)* (= not be fair)	*What a rip-off! He charged me ten dollars* * too much.*
trick someone **into** + VERB*ing* (= use dishonest ways to make someone do something)	*She tricked me into telling her my age.*
deceive someone **about** something (= make a person believe what is not true)	*They deceived us about the money.*
con someone **into** { + VERB*ing* something *(slang)* (= trick someone)	*He conned me into* { *buying a used car for a* * high price.* *a card game.*
pull a fast one on someone *(slang)* (= trick someone)	*That guy really pulled a fast one on me; he sold* * me a car without an engine.*

▦▦▦▦ TELLING THE STORY

A. Look at the picture story. Underline the correct word(s) to complete each sentence.

EXAMPLE: The gangster is (sure / <u>not sure</u>) about the address.

---

1. The gangster (trusts / distrusts) the jewelry salesperson.
2. After he leaves, the gangster starts to (believe / doubt) that the diamond is real.
3. The jeweler across the street says that the diamond is (real / fake).
4. The salesperson decides that the money is (real / counterfeit).
5. Both men were (honest / dishonest) with each other.
6. Both men were (telling the truth / lying) about calling the police.
7. Both men started laughing because they had tried to (cheat / be honest with) each other.
8. It's (legal / illegal) to cheat other people.

B. How well did you understand the story? Don't look at the pictures.
Write **T** if the statement is **true**, **F** if it is **false**.

EXAMPLE: _F_ The gangster was sure about the address.

---

1. _____ The gangster didn't trust the salesperson.
2. _____ From the beginning, the gangster suspected that the diamond might be fake.
3. _____ The salesperson didn't trust the gangster.
4. _____ The salesperson thought that the money might be counterfeit.
5. _____ The jeweler said that the diamond was fake.
6. _____ Both men were telling the truth about calling the police.
7. _____ It's legal* to cheat someone.
8. _____ Both the salesperson and the gangster were honest people.

C. Work with a partner. Explain or correct the false statements.

EXAMPLE: [say] **The example is false. He wasn't sure about the address.**

_____

*legal (adj.) = allowed by law

▓▓▓▓ BODY LANGUAGE

A. Match each picture with a description of the action. Write the correct letter on the line.

1. _____ stand with one's mouth open

2. _____ raise one's eyebrows

3. _____ scratch one's head

4. _____ not look someone in the eye

5. _____ cross one's fingers behind one's back
   (= gesture made when someone is telling a lie)

B. Work in pairs. Cover the words. Look only at the pictures. Describe what each person is doing and why. (Make up your explanations.)

EXAMPLE: Picture E
  1. **What's she doing?   She's standing with her mouth open.**
  2. **Why?   ...because somebody just cheated her.**
          ...because somebody just played a trick on her.

C. In groups, talk about cultural differences. Answer these questions:

1. Do people in your culture show their disbelief in the same way as in the pictures?

2. How do they act when they think someone is lying to them?

3. How do they act when they think someone is cheating them?

4. In what other ways do people express doubt or uncertainty in your culture?

Summarize your discussion for the class.

▦▦▦▦ EXPRESSIONS AND CONVERSATIONS

A. Practice the following conversation with your partner. Use the appropriate body language to act out (dramatize) the situation.

A: I'm sure that the bus will be on time today!

B: Oh, yeah? Well, I doubt it. It's never on time.

A: Oh, come on. It might be different today. I heard that there is a new driver.

B: Well, in that case, you might be right. Maybe we should try to think positively.

B. Now practice the conversation again. Use different expressions for the underlined words. Have several different conversations.

EXAMPLE: [instead of] I doubt it.
              [say] **I don't think so.**

▦ Expressing Doubt

I doubt it.
I don't think so.

I'm not so sure.
Don't count on it.

▦ Expressing Possibility

It **might** be different.
It **may** be early.

In that case, you **might** be right.
If that's true, you **may** be right.

C. Practice the following conversation with your partner.

WAITRESS: How old are you?

CUSTOMER: Twenty-one.

WAITRESS: <u>You're kidding!</u> You know something...<u>I don't believe you!</u>

CUSTOMER: What's the matter? <u>Don't I have an honest face?</u>

WAITRESS: You look very young. That's why <u>I'm not sure that you're telling the truth.</u> Let's see your I.D.*

CUSTOMER: *(taking out wallet)* <u>Believe me! I'm telling the truth.</u>

Practice the conversation again. Use expressions from the following list instead of the underlined words.

▩ **Expressing Disbelief**

I don't believe you!
You're putting me on! *(slang)*

You're { **kidding!**
        { **joking!**

I'm not sure that you're telling the truth.
I'm not convinced that you're being honest.

You're lying. *(very strong)*

▩ **Expressing Honesty**

Believe me!	**I'm telling the truth.**
Trust me!	**I'm not lying.**

Don't I have an honest face?
Do I look dishonest?

*I.D. (n.) = identification

D. Practice the following conversation with your partner.

ROCK STAR: Do you know who I am? <u>Believe me</u>, you're making a big mistake!

POLICE OFFICER: <u>As a matter of fact</u>, I don't care who you are. If you <u>break the law</u>, I have to arrest* you.

ROCK STAR: I want to call my lawyer†. You can't do this to me!

POLICE OFFICER: Look, if you <u>do something illegal</u>, you go to jail††. That's the way it is. It doesn't matter who you are!

Practice the conversation again. Use expressions from the following list instead of the underlined words.

▨ **Expressing Belief** (= when you are sure something is true, not false)

Believe me,...	**As a matter of fact,**...
You can be sure,...	**To tell the truth,**...
In fact,...	
Actually,...	

▨ **Describing Dishonest Behavior**

You { **break the law**... / **commit a crime**...

You do **something** { **illegal.** / **against the law.** / **criminal.**

E. Now role play the situations in this section. Use your own words and the appropriate body language. How do you feel in each situation?

---

*arrest (v.) = hold a suspected criminal
†lawyer (n.) = professional who gives advice about the law
††jail (n.) = place where criminals are locked up

▦▦▦▦ EXPRESSING YOURSELF

What Do You Say? Use these expressions in your answers to the questions that follow.

EXPRESSIONS

You tricked me.

Is it a fake?

That's cheating!

I doubt it.

Why did you deceive me?

He looks suspicious.

He's lying!

That guy's a crook.

I wonder if she's right.

EXAMPLE: What do you say when someone sells you a TV that doesn't work?
[say] **You tricked me.**

A. WHAT DO YOU SAY?

1. ...when your boyfriend or girlfriend tells you that he or she is already married?

2. ...when a friend tells you she paid someone to take a test for her?

3. ...when you see a man sitting in a car in front of your apartment building several times in one week?

4. ...when a friend gives you some advice about your life?

5. ...when someone wants to sell "an original Picasso painting" for $50?

6. ...when you're describing a businessman who always cheats his customers?

7. ...when you hear a politician making impossible promises on TV?

8. ...when someone asks you if you can stop talking for one day?

⬛⬛⬛⬛ ROLE PLAY

Work with a partner.
Choose one of the following situations.
Each student plays one role.
Read and think only about your role.
How do you feel?
Act out the situations. Use expressions from this chapter.
(Your teacher may ask a third student to direct and give suggestions.)

Role A	Role B
1. You are the security officer at a supermarket. You explain to an older person that you must arrest him for shoplifting (stealing) food.	1. You are the older shopper. The officer arrests you, but you complain loudly that you didn't do anything illegal.
2. You are ordering fish at a small family restaurant. You tell the owner that you doubt that the fish is fresh.	2. You are both the owner of the restaurant and the cook. You just went fishing yesterday, and you have to convince the customer that the fish is fresh.
3. You just met a person who said he can read minds*. When you doubted him, he told you secrets about yourself and your friend. You tell your friend the story about the mindreader.	3. You are the friend. You don't believe your friend's story until he tells you a secret about yourself. Then you start to believe in the mindreader.
4. Someone just tricked you and sold you a broken TV set. You feel stupid because you didn't trust the person but you bought the set anyway. You tell the story to a friend.	4. You listen to your friend's story. Then you tell your own story about buying a used car from a dishonest used car dealer.
5. (your own situation) ?	5. (your own situation) ?

---

*read minds = tell what other people are thinking

▓▓▓▓ INTERVIEW

Ask your partner the following questions. Take notes on the answers. (Your teacher may ask you to do this exercise in groups of three or four.)

1. What kind of salesperson do you distrust the most?

_____

EXAMPLE: [say] **I distrust used car salespeople the most.**

2. People often distrust politicians and their promises. Name one politician you don't trust. Explain why.
3. Has anyone ever tried to cheat you? Explain what happened.
4. In your opinion, should a teacher punish a student who cheats on an exam? Why or why not? If so, how?
5. Can you tell if someone is lying? How? Have you ever lied about your age? Where and why?
6. Have you ever told a "white lie" (a small lie about an unimportant matter)? Give an example. Why did you tell it?
7. It is illegal to drive without a license. Name four other things that are illegal.
8. Compare the attitude toward honesty in your country to the attitude here (for example, honesty in advertising, in business deals). In which country are people generally more honest, in your opinion? What about people in government?

Now change partners. Ask your new partner the same questions about his or her first partner. Use the third person, as in this example:

_____

EXAMPLE: What kind of salespeople does she distrust the most?
       [say] **She distrusts used car salespeople the most.**

❑❑❑❑ ONE STEP FURTHER

Gᴀᴍᴇ: "I ᴅᴏᴜʙᴛ ɪᴛ!"

You will need 3″ by 5″ cards for this game.

1. On one side of the card, write something that you know how to do very well.

_____

EXAMPLE:[write] I know how to speak Japanese very well.

_____

2. On the other side of the card, you have to tell a lie. Write that you know how to do something that you *don't* know how to do, but that you *would like to learn* to do.

_____

EXAMPLE:[write] I know how to fly an airplane very well.

_____

3. Take turns. Each student reads his or her statements to the class. The class must decide if the statements are true or false.

4. If you think the statement is true, say, "I believe it!" If you think it is false, say, "I doubt it!" Afterwards, the student who wrote the false statement must correct it.

_____

EXAMPLE:[say] **You're right. I don't know how to fly an airplane.**

_____

5. If you want to make the game more difficult, mix up the cards before you begin. First guess whose card it is. Then decide if it is true or false.

▧▧▧▧ PROBLEM SOLVING

Read the situation and possible solutions to yourself.
Which is the best solution? Write 1 next to the best idea, 2 next to the
  second best idea, and so forth.
Then work in groups of three or four.
Choose a secretary for your group.
Discuss your answers. Decide as a group the best order of the solutions.
The group secretary may write down the numbers.
Compare the answers of the different groups in the class.
Discuss why you chose certain solutions.

SITUATION: A salesperson calls to congratulate you on winning a "free"
trip to Hawaii. Then he or she explains that you must attend a sales
presentation to qualify for the trip. You are not sure if you should take
time off work to go to the presentation.

WHAT SHOULD YOU DO?

a. _____ Hang up immediately. Wonder if you missed a chance for a
free trip.

b. _____ Believe the salesperson is telling the truth. Tell all your friends
you're going to Hawaii. Take time off from work, even if it
upsets your boss.

c. _____ Be very suspicious of the offer of a "free" trip. Ask for the
complete name of the company and manager. If the salesperson
refuses to give this information, say "No, thank you" and hang
up.

d. _____ Before deciding, ask the salesperson if you must buy something
to win the trip. Then contact the Better Business Bureau to find
out if there have been complaints about the company.

e. _____ Explain that you are very busy and don't have time to attend
the sales presentation. Ask the salesperson to send you
information about the trip in the mail. If he or she says that is
impossible, say goodbye politely and hang up.

f. _____ (your own solution)_____

_____

_____

▦▦▦▦ WORDPLAY

A. **Prepositions.** Complete the story with the correct prepositions. Use *of, to, with, at, into,* or *about.*

Dear Ms. A. D. Vice,

I hope you can give me some advice. I'm having a lot of trouble with my girlfriend, and I'm not sure ___*about*___ what to do. Here is the problem:
₁

When I tell her I'm working late at the office, she never **believes** me. She always **suspects** me _____ lying _____
₂ ₃
little things. Of course, I am never **dishonest** _____ her!
₄
(Well, maybe once or twice I **lied** _____ her
₅
_____ other women.)
₆

Last weekend she tried to **cheat** me _____ cards.
₇
Then she **tricked** me _____ buying her a ring! She never
₈
acted like that before! When I ask her if something is wrong, she just says, "No, why?"

I don't think she's being **honest** _____ me _____
₉ ₁₀
her feelings. Maybe she's **deceiving** me _____ other things,
₁₁
too. What should I do? Please help me!

Sincerely,
Worried and Confused

DISCUSSION (optional)

1. What do you think this man should do?

2. Have you ever been worried and confused about someone's behavior? Who did you ask for advice?

B. **Sentence Completion.** Make sentences from these words. Add prepositions and other words you need. Use the past or past continuous tense, as appropriate.

EXAMPLE: gangster/ not be / sure / if / he / have / right address

[write]   *The gangster was not sure if he had the right address.*

---

1. when / he / buy / diamond, / he / wonder / price

2. after / he / leave / store, / he / doubt / that / diamond / be / real

3. salesperson / and / gangster / do / not trust / each other

4. jeweler / examine / diamond / and / decide / that / it / be / fake

5. after / gangster / leave, / salesperson / realize / money / be / counterfeit / too

6. they / both / lie / each other / and / try / cheat / each other

---

C. **Parts of Speech.** Complete the story. Use the correct forms of the words.

Each year on April 15, you must pay your income tax in the United States. Most taxpayers try to be honest; however, they don't want to pay more than is necessary.

---

cheating = noun   **cheat** = verb   **dishonestly** = adverb

---

1. Cheating _____ on your income tax is illegal.
2. But most taxpayers doubt that they will be caught if they _____ a little on their income tax.
3. So each year thousands of taxpayers fill out their forms _____ .

---

false = adjective   **lie** = verb   **falsely** = adverb

---

4. Last year, Ted Smirk, a rich businessman, wrote down
   _____ information on his income-tax form.

5. He _____ about his income.

6. He stated _____ that he had lost money.

---

suspicious = adjective   **suspect** = verb   **suspiciously** = adverb

---

7. At first the government didn't _____ him of doing
   anything wrong.

8. Then an income-tax official became _____ of Smirk
   after reading an article about him in the newspaper.

9. Smirk acted _____ when the official asked him a few
   questions, so the official ordered an investigation.

---

law = noun   **lawyer** = noun (person)   **illegal** = adjective

---

10. It is _____ to give false information to the
    government.

11. The _____ says that you must go to jail or pay extra
    money if you cheat on your income tax.

12. Recently, Smirk received an official letter from a _____
    for the Internal Revenue Service.* It said that he must go to court.

DISCUSSION (optional)

1. Why do citizens pay income taxes to their governments?

2. Do citizens in your country pay income tax? Do some people try to
   cheat?

3. In your opinion, does your government collect a fair amount of
   taxes from its citizens?

4. Should governments punish citizens who cheat on their taxes? If so,
   how?

---

*Internal Revenue Service = branch of the United States government that collects taxes

▓▓▓▓ ANSWER KEY

EXPRESSING YOURSELF EXERCISES

Note: More than one answer may be appropriate.

CHAPTER 1

Exercise C — **What Do You Say?** (p.10)
1. Did you enjoy your trip?
2. Congratulations! Let's go celebrate.
3. Boy, are you lucky!
4. We're very proud of you!
5. I'm delighted to meet you!
6. I'm thrilled.
7. I feel great!
8. What an accomplishment!

CHAPTER 3

Exercise A — **What Do You Say?** (p. 42)
1. It's a riot/hilarious!
2. You're putting me on . . .
3. Are you being sarcastic?
4. She cracks me up.
5. I'm insulted.
6. That's ridiculous.
7. Don't be silly.
8. How embarrassing!

CHAPTER 4

Exercise B — **What Do You Do?** (p. 58)
1. I lose my temper.
2. I get nervous.
3. I apologize.
4. I get upset.
5. I complain.
6. I argue.
7. I get angry.
8. I blame him.
9. We discuss it.

CHAPTER 5

Exercise A - **What Should You Do?** (p. 74)
1. f   2. a   3. i   4. c   5. h   6. b
7. d   8. e

CHAPTER 6

Exercise A — **What Do You Say?** (p.89)
1. Don't hesitate to call me.
2. That gave me the creeps.
3. Don't panic!
4. It shocked all of us!
5. Why are you so nervous?
6. I'm dreading every minute of it.
7. How strange . . .
8. What a tragic story!

CHAPTER 7

Exercise A — **What Do You Say?** (p. 106)
1. Would you care for something else?
2. How considerate of you!
3. I'm very grateful for your help.
4. Did he ask you out yet?
5. I really appreciate it.
6. I'm very fond of this place.
7. Are you still in love?
8. How are you getting along?

CHAPTER 8

Exercise A — **What Do You Say?** (p. 121)
1. We don't get along.
2. I really regret that.
3. I can't stand it anymore.
4. I'm jealous.
5. I don't like to hold grudges.
6. I'll get even with you!
7. You hurt my feelings.
8. Why are you ignoring me?

Exercise B — **How Do You Act or Feel?** (p. 122)
1. I get jealous.
2. I don't like it.
3. I avoid it.
4. I hate it.
5. I complain.
6. I ignore it.
7. I dislike it.

Express Yourself!

CHAPTER 9

Exercise A — **What Do You Say?** (p. 139)
1. Don't be such a sucker!
2. Can I count on you?
3. Promise not to tell anyone?
4. I can't make up my mind.
5. Have confidence in yourself!
6. I'll be frank with you.
7. You're so naive . . .
8. I swear I didn't do it.

CHAPTER 10

Exercise A — **What Do You Say?** (p. 157)
1. Why did you deceive me?
2. That's cheating!
3. He looks suspicious.
4. I wonder if she's right.
5. Is it fake?
6. That guy's a crook.
7. He's lying!
8. I doubt it.